"All we do is talk steel"
Oral Histories of Sparrows Point

By Bill Barry

© by Bill Barry   2019

Others books by this author are:
I Just Got Elected, Now What: The New Union Officers' Handbook (2nd edition)
The 1877 Railroad Strike in Baltimore
Union Strategies for Hard Times (2nd edition)
From First Contact to First Contract: A Union Organizer's Handbook (3rd Edition)
Closing Up the Open Shop: A Guide to Internal Organizing
Don't Trump on Us: Making Our Unions Great Again

Send all comments and correspondence to:

4204 Elsrode Avenue
Baltimore, MD 21214-3107
Billbarry21214@gmail.com

In Memory of
Mark McCulloch
Steelworker historian and friend

"When we got together with our families, when we get together now –we talk steel. All we do is talk steel, how to make it better, how to do this, how to do that, try to come up with answers, how to make the union better, how to make everything better, always trying to make something better."

Edie Papadakis Butler

TABLE OF CONTENTS

Chapter 1—Neal Crowder p. 1
Chapter 2—Mugs Rytter p. 17
Chapter 3—Lee Douglass p. 21
Chapter 4—Joe Kotelchuck p. 39
Chapter 5—Edie Papadakis Butler p. 53
Chapter 6—Eddie Bartee, Sr. p. 62
Chapter 7—Mary Lorenzo p. 78
Chapter 8—LeRoy McClelland p. 98
Glossary p. 139
Afterword p. 142

Neal Crowder
February, 2004

I was born in Philadelphia. I lost my parents early, ya know, and I was farmed out to relatives. I lived down in Edgemere at Lynch Point for seven years with an aunt and uncle and then I went back to Philadelphia again. We had a falling out and they sent me back. I was 14 then and I stayed in Philly until I was 17. I had to quit school – ten and a half grades –and went to work for Western Union as a telegraph messenger. So I did that for a year. And after that – it was bitter cold in the winter out there on a bike, ya know – and I decided to go back down to Sparrows Point again to see if I could get a job. I didn't get one right away. I had to work at a restaurant for a couple of weeks and at a box factory.

So my uncle got a letter written for me by the guy that was head of the VFW in Edgemere down there. And he wrote one of those tear-jerker letters, ya know. He says: *Please give this young man, an orphan, a job.* So it worked, I got hired. I was 17; I told them I was 19.

And my uncle--I was living with him and we had a terrible relationship. I guess I was fiercely independent. My aunt wanted to take care of my money for me and I said, "No, I'm gonna take care of my money myself." So I'd go back and forth staying with her. Ya know, you have these attachments, but it never worked out. When I finally got married in '41, we were ready to fall out again, but I was with them until then.

So I got hired in down there. That was 1936, September the 10th. I got the stubs to prove it. Well it's hard for me to really remember my first day. If I answered that question, I'd probably be making something up 'cause I actually don't remember how I felt anymore. The best I could say is that it really overwhelmed me going in there the first day.

I had a really bumpy career with Bethlehem Steel because I was the kind of kid that would speak up a lot, ya know. I had something blamed on me one night. I had no part of what happened but the foreman was looking for somebody to blame. I was the crane follower and I had to keep the shears in the strip mill supplied with steel, 20 minutes, and then at another mill. Well it took an hour and ten minutes to pull the work rolls from the mill, and everything went down and he blamed it on me. And I tried to reason with him, but I couldn't reason with him. Before it was over, I even tried to provoke him into a fight, but he didn't buy that, he was too smart. He was about 40 years old, which to a kid of 17 is an old guy, ya know what I mean?

So anyway, this helped make a union guy out of me. I could see the injustices in the place. Of course, I couldn't join the union then; there wasn't any. But anyway, they sent me to the assistant superintendent. He was the guy who run the mill. The superintendent made the bullets, but this guy fired them. His name was Johnny Edwards. They called him "The Bulldog." They docked my pay, my fabulous pay – 42 and a half cents an hour at 5 o'clock in the morning on the day turn. And of course, I had to wait around to see him when I walked in his office. I identified myself and he said to me: "I don't want to hear a word you have to say." He said, "My foreman told me what's going on. I'm sending you back to the employment office." So that's what he did – we had unit seniority back in those days – it cost me a year of unit seniority because they put me back in the labor gang. I'd only been there two months when this happened too, ya know. But anyway, I never forgot what he said to me. I figured that anyone who won't listen to the other person's side of the story, I don't have much use for them. And I never had any use for him, even though later on, I had to deal with him as a union shop steward and he didn't mess with me anymore.

Well it was a kind of a scary place to be in. You know you look up and see these huge cranes going overhead carrying loads of steel and stuff. It was awesome for me to be in a place like that. The most dangerous thing I had done was ride the bike in Philly, which was dangerous enough.

When I was hired in 1936, I went into the 42- and 48-inch cold reducing mill; that was essentially the tin plate mill. Well they had a tandem mill and the tandem mills are strand mills. When it's going into the mill it's about one-sixteenth of an inch thick. When it's coming out of that mill, the first strands are just moving--these five strands. But when it's coming out, it's flying – four thousand feet a minute, ya know. It's really something to watch. So that was my experience on that and after that, they would take it over to what they called the washer department. In fact, I hated to work in there. When I was working in the labor gang I'd get sent in there to fill in and it would make my skin itch because they used caustic soda in the tanks. And I thought, "Oh God." When I finally went to get a job, he had forgotten who I was – it was a year later – and he said, "I got just the job for you, in the washer room." But you know I didn't have any choice. I had to take it but I spent 19 years in there. That's where I spent all my union organizing.

There was no union talk at all in there. There was no talk about unions until a guy like me got into it at, say, the end of '39 or '40. I don't remember any talk [about the union] when I came in in 1936 but it was going on. It was going on in the pipe mills and they were having some wild times over there too, ya know, between the Bethlehem police and the people, the pipe mills and the wire mill and all that over there. But they weren't getting in our place. The closest I can show you – I got old union cards showing the dollar stamps. They're mine personally, but I would also sign people up. The fact of the matter, they said, "For every guy you sign up you get a dollar." Well the dues were a dollar. So when I would get a non-member, I'd say, "OK, I'll pay your first month dues for you." So I never took the money. I used it as an inducement to pay their dues even though it was a buck. A buck then was worth a lot more money back then.

I think there was more activity in the pipe mill and the wire mill because maybe the conditions were worse over there. I think some of them started [organizing] as early as '37. But they didn't get over to our place.

I can tell you a little story about how I came to join the union. As close as I can tell I was probably 20 years old then. So I'd worked there three years, I guess. So I was getting a hair cut up on Conkling Street and it was a union barber in there. He said to me, "Hey kid, where do you work?" I said, "Bethlehem Steel, Sparrows Point." He said, "Do you belong to the union?" I laughed and said, "Man, I don't know anything about unions at all." Well he said the Steelworkers Organizing Committee – that's the SWOC – was started by the mineworkers under John L Lewis. And he said they had offices over Wonder Clothes up there, a suite of offices. And he said, "Why don't you go down and join the union." So, I said, "Boy, it sounds like a good idea to me." So, I did. And there were guys 40 or 50 years old, mineworkers, I guess. They almost hugged and kissed me. Oh, here's what the barber said, he said, "They want to get people inside the mills because they'd give leaflets out and people would just throw them away."

It seemed to me that, when I was signing people up, I never run into a lot of difficulty. The worst I had was that I signed up seven that time and the boss decided to fire all of us. Of course, he retracted it but that played right into my hands in signing them up. Yeah, I took the cards up to the office at Paca Street and Eastern Avenue. In fact, when I got back out of the Navy, I went up and visited them at the office and the one mineworker, he calls in one of the other guys and said, "Hey look. This guy used to really sign people up."

So they made me a shop steward and gave me a book for being a shop steward and a bunch of little buttons. And I signed up... Oh I was really signing them up, ya know. But we were not wearing the buttons yet. Back then we didn't wear hard hats. We just wore a little train hat or something to keep your head clean. So after I got it really organized, one morning we came in on the 8 to 4 [shift] and I said, "Ok, put your buttons on today." And I led a lot of revolts. They would tell you, "Here, you're working the production line." And they'd tell you you'd have to clean up, sweep up, while the coil's running. And the first thing I did when – we didn't have a signed contract – the first thing I did when we got organized, I said to the guys – now I wasn't the operator but I was a welder in the back – I said, "When they bring that broom around..." The boss wasn't a bad guy, the general foreman, but he was the kind of guy that stuck his lip out and he'd take the broom and give it to you. I said, "Now the first thing I'm gonna do is throw it over in the corner. Now if he comes to each one of you, you do the same thing, because if you don't, they're gonna come back to me and say, 'Well, you're the only one who did it.'" Well it worked. I threw it over in the corner and told him, "From now on, have a laborer come in and sweep this place. We're not gonna do that anymore." So, he saw the writing on the wall, so you didn't have to take stuff further than that.

But I tell you, Johnny Edwards, the Bulldog helped me. I had seven guys who wouldn't join the union. By this time, we're up around '41 or '42. We didn't have the election until '42. It was conducted in the mill under the auspices of the federal government, the Labor Department. So, he had jerked a whole bunch of us in the office one day. Back in those days, they would run a lot of steel in bulk. They'd put it in tiers and then cover that, then they'd have a big house come over on top of it. Then they put gas to it. Well when they run in a tandem mill, they run it through a box annealing so when it's going in, it's not just being elongated, it's widening out too. If they didn't set the boxes up right, it squeezed the thing and put what they call a ridge through the center.

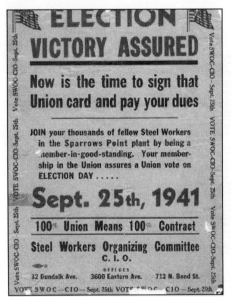

And I knew when he called us in, he was gonna chew everybody out. Now I'm only about 22 years old at this time. And it's an amazing thing. We had a little place in the mill, we called it the dog house. That's where they brought you in to chew you out – a little steel building in the building. They'd line you up against the wall like they were gonna shoot you, ya know what I mean? They didn't say, "Sit down, fellas." It was nothing like that. So, when they started out about the order being messed up, nobody spoke up but me. And I said, "Well, Mr. Edwards . . ." Back then I call him Mr. Edwards. When I came out of the Navy, I dropped the mister stuff. I'd had enough of that. I said, "Well Mr. Edwards, it seems to me that if everybody in here run it and everybody made that order stick, it seems to me it was in the order, it had a ridge in it." And here's what he said to me – this guy helped me all the time be a good union guy – he said, "Listen, you're just a green operator" – but I knew what I was doing – "and you'll never operate again." And he said, "And I don't want you to have any more to say in here." I said, "Well, Mr. Edwards, you're running the show so if you say I can't speak in here, I can't. But as far as me not operating again, we'll see about that."

And even though we didn't have a signed contract, I went and got the zone committeeman and they rammed me right back down his throat again. But I had seven guys I couldn't sign up in the union and he told us, "I'm gonna suspend all of youse." When we got to the doorway leading out to the tandem mill he must of thought, "I've made a mistake." He called us all back, but he helped me out. I went around and signed all seven. I said, "You just lost your job without the union, that's all you can lose." So, I signed the seven up on the turn.

But there was other times, he'd call you in when we were really organizing. They had an independent union that was backed by the company. They wanted to put this independent union in there, ya know. The word was they had fixed one of these stand-up desks between our departments for them to sign people up. So he calls me off my job one day and says to me – now I'm not sitting down, there's no invitation, it's all stand up. He says "I hear you've been soliciting membership for your union." I'd already been wised up what to say by higher ups in the union, but they didn't tell me what I was gonna say. And I said, "Yes Mr. Edwards. You know what, I hear the company has OK'd – you have OK'd – a desk for the independent union to sign up." And he didn't know what I was talking about but I knew that was true. I says, "I'll tell you what, that's against the National Labor Relations Act." I wasn't even sure it was. And I said, "I'll tell you right now, if you do the same thing for us, if you give us a desk, I won't say a word about the other thing for the independent union." They even had a flunky run around in there and do nothing. He was for the independent union, he was one of our mechanics. And he tried to talk to me about it. He was a much older guy than me. I guess he must have been 40 years old. Anyway, he said, "Look I've had bad experiences with the union," and stuff like that. And I told him – his name was Webb – I said, "Chuck, you're wasting your time with me. I'm not gonna mess with your independent union at all. I don't think much of it."

When I first started working, I lived in Lynch Point, part of Edgemere. That's where I lived with my aunt and uncle. I was always in that area, but sometimes I boarded with other people. After I got married, we stayed in that area for… Well when we first got married, my wife, her mother had had a heart attack and a stroke, so we lived with them. We didn't have much money anyway ourselves, ya know. I think I might have been making 75 cents an hour at the welding job I did. So, then we pitched in together with them and bought a house up in Cedarcrest. That's where we were living and things got so bad with my wife, she was pregnant and all that, we went for a while into an apartment. But then her mom died. She felt so bad, we moved back with her dad. But then I was drafted in the Navy and we had to give it all up. My wife wound up in Massachusetts for about a year and half during my Navy service – I was in the Navy for two years and four months – but she wound up there with relatives. That was a big help for her. It was my home port for a couple months, but not long.

Many times, things came up and I spoke up, even before I went in the Navy. I worked seven years there before I went into the Navy. And the general foreman of my department said… Ya know, back then they would give deferments for people for six months. Well I had a wife and a baby, four months old, and I would have taken it. But the day I reported to the draft board in Dundalk – a one room draft board – and the woman who run the place, I asked her, "If Bethlehem Steel put in a deferment for me, would you have a record of it?" She said "Yes." Because I'm curious, ya know. So, she looked through a little metal can, it looked like a recipe can. She said,

"No, there's nothing here." And I said, "I didn't expect there would be." So anyway, I went away for two years and four months.

I was everywhere in the Navy. Everywhere. Let me show you where I was. [He holds up campaign hat that reads "USS Cronin DE- 704"] This ribbon here represents China service. After the war ended, we escorted troop transports and an aircraft carrier up to Korea and China for the occupation. This one down here is the occupation medal. It's got an Asia clasp on it. This is for taking part in the liberation of the Philippines, it's called the Philippines Liberation medal. And this is the Philippines Independence medal. Both these medals were granted by the Philippine government, not us. This one here is European-Africa-Middle East. This is Asiatic Pacific. This is American Theater, whether you stayed in port or went up and down the coast line. This is the World War II Victory medal. This is what they called the ruptured duck, when you got out.

My wife was from Baltimore City. She was born in Massachusetts and came here when she was an infant. They moved down to the country because her dad had been an old country guy from up in Michigan – French descent, but not a French speaker. She was always good with me about everything. She always went along with everything. It was a tumultuous life, ya know, with the union and stuff. There was always some agitation or aggravation going on. They're threatening to fire me or something.

We took a bus trip not long ago – two bus trips – for union retirees over to Washington. Well, they get you out of the bus and people come up and speak to you. A guy from the head of the Commerce Department spoke one time. Of course, we know what's happened now – Bush caved in to the international court and lifted tariffs. So, I just hope it works out good, ya know what I mean? It was mostly rallies. Go over there to jack [President George] Bush, up to let him know what the steelworkers thought. But I guess they didn't want to pay the big fines either, so they decided to cave into them.

But before we left, Len Shindell, a very nice fellow, he was the bus captain for us. Marian Wilson said to him while he's recognizing all these union people, and I'm 20 years their senior so nobody knows me, none of the older ones were on my bus. But Marian spoke up and said, "There's someone else on this bus that helped put the union in here." So, he had me come up and use the mic and I was telling them stories. I said, "Bethlehem Steel helped me get in the Navy. I never been able to thank them for that. Now they're in bankruptcy and I can't write them a nice letter telling them how much I appreciated it. They scuttled our health benefits, right? But see, I'm a veteran and I'm entitled to the VA. Without their help I'd have never got it if they would have deferred me. But they figured they were gonna get rid of a big trouble maker. And they did, for two years and four months." But I said, "You know what? I came back to haunt them for 37 more years."

For the union election [in September, 1941], they had all these tables up in the mill and you came in and voted. Yeah, it was quite a thing. Yes, I remember that. The vote count was overwhelming.

Everybody was happy about it. Oh, I'll tell you a little story that a friend of mine who worked in the mill said to me. He was an older fellow than me and he said, "You know what the union did for us, Neal?" I said, "What?" He said, "Well it keeps the boss from coming up and cocking his leg and pissing on your leg like a dog. They can't do that anymore." You know in one interview I had – my wife had a stroke and they wanted to interview me – and they came down to my yard. I forget who did it. But anyway, they asked me that: "What do you think the greatest thing that the union did?" And I said without hesitation, "It put democracy in the work place and gave us independence, which we didn't have." Just the thing of calling you in and chewing you out: "Don't sit down, just everybody stand up." Bethlehem Steel, I'd say they were a pretty autocratic employer, ya know.

Steelworkers voting for the union in September, 1941

People would say it's hard to get fired from Bethlehem Steel. That was basically true, too. But they did so many things against black people. Of course, back in those days, there was collaboration with the union. The only bad thing I can say about the union was that they – it wasn't in the higher ups but in the lower levels – they would set up units the way they did it in my mill and the way I think they did all over Sparrows Point. They would set up units of seniority. So you didn't go by plant seniority, you went by unit seniority. That's the way they kept the black person down. It was done that way. No use for me naming names. Of course, I knew who the zone committeeman was at that time. But he's dead and gone so it doesn't do any good to name names. But I know that's how he felt, and he helped set those things up with the superintendent, who was David Stringer at that time.

You know I lived through just about every superintendent they had down there. I went over to a meeting for salary people. I was interviewed by a girl, Christine something, from the Sun paper, up at the union hall at one of our meetings or dinners. We spent an hour together. In fact, I didn't even eat. Then she never used any of it. And I just felt it was an affront. I wrote her a long letter and everything, ya know. Whoever told her to come see Neal, I think it was Don Kellner. And everybody said to her, "You're talking to the right guy, he can tell you stuff." And I said to her, "Why didn't you stop the interview if you weren't gonna use it?" I left stuff on her voice mail and wrote a letter to the editor too objecting to the way she was with me. And she said, "Well I just didn't want to interrupt you." I said, "There's such a thing as integrity and that's what you're gonna have to learn." I'm talking to a young person, ya know.

I gave up the shop steward job in 1965, although I kept my hand in the incentive stuff because the union wanted me too. Don Kellner got me to do that. And I said to the Sun reporter, "Ya know, a superintendent came up to me… I'm running the big line; it's still there, on Bethlehem Boulevard there. It's a big building, eight stories high and a city block long. It's an awesome sight. It's awesome when it breaks too. Anyway, he came up to me and I was under the furnace watching the strip exit before it went to the loop, and he said, "Neal…" And when I'm telling her this story I said, "It's odd but I think the greatest compliment I ever received was from him in management." And the superintendent he says to me, "Well, the people have lost a good representative." And then he looked at me and said, "Well Neal, you weren't always the easiest guy to get along with but you always kept your word." I said to her, "That means a lot."

I've also been given another compliment. This is really something. This is by a friend of mine, a black fellow, John Parker. They had things tied up so bad that the black people couldn't get jobs; they couldn't get in the unit. Well, I found out I could get them jobs on tractors and cranes and in the electrical department and I would go down there. I saw the man in charge and he'd give a job to every guy I brought down there. So, John Parker says to me a couple years ago at one of our union meetings for retirees, he said, "Hey Neal, You know what they used to call you?" I said, "No, John. What?" Oh, if one of our white guys would go to a black guy and say who's a good shop steward, they'd say, "Go to the nigger-loving shop steward Crowder." I said to John, "You know what?

It's a lousy term to be used but in this case I regard it as a compliment."

For my attitude, well for one thing I went to school under both systems, at Sparrows Point High School with segregation and then I went to school in Philly, which was integrated. Listen, this is really something. I left Sparrows Point High School and went to South Philadelphia High School, same letters. But they put me back a whole year because I left the 8th grade which was high school down here – they only had 11 grades of high school – and I went up there and my aunt took me down to the high school office and told the principal I should go in the 9th grade, the first year of high school up there. And the principal said, "No, we'll put him in 8B. They might have been right but it put me back a whole year. I think it made me quit school sooner because I know I had to go longer. I think you know I didn't have that feeling against black people I guess because I was treated unjustly myself often in the mills. See, when you got hired back then, if you weren't somebody's friend or relative, you were nobody. Once that letter cleared the way to hire me, I had no influence, nothing, ya know what I mean? So I was always in trouble. I guess I figured being the underdog I could sympathize with them.

I'd get pretty wound with some bosses. I represented a young fellow one day. He was a white young fellow, but he said he belonged back in the washer unit and they put him in box anneal department. So, I went over to see the assistant superintendent. He didn't like me either; I was too outspoken, I guess. You rub a lot fur when you don't always agree with people. So, I brought this up, and he was a big man. He had been a former football player in Indiana in college. He wasn't a bad guy, he just didn't like me. Jeff James was his name. I walked in his office. I forgot why he had taken an initial dislike for me. It could have been for different reasons because I battle for anybody who's being shafted real bad.

So, when I walked into his office, I introduced the young fellow and I said, "Jeff, this young fellow feels he belongs back in the washer department." And James was in a real bad mood that day, I guess. And he stood up behind his desk – he reminded me of King Kong or something – and he says to me, "Why don't you just come in here and run this place." And I said, "Well if I could do a damn better job than you're doing, I think I could handle it." Well that isn't going to placate him, right? He actually looked like he could strangle me. The phone rang and I thought, "This is a good time to exit." So while he's on the phone and he can't even answer me I said to the young fellow – and I'm gonna to use the language that we used – I said "Let's go. We don't have to listen to any more of this shit." And I said. "But we'll be back." And I did return and within a couple of weeks, I brought the zone committeeman back and he told him in no uncertain terms, "We don't give a damn whether you like Neal or not, but when he comes in here you show proper respect for the shop steward." So, he was a little better after that.

I shut the whole washer department down on him one day. I had a young fellow, now this was in 1950, and he had just come back out of the Korean War, and he limped along. He had been shot in the heel over there. His name was Kirkpatrick or something. I looked at him and it's a little after 8 o'clock and he's walking with his lunch box. And I said, "Where you going Kip?" Oh he says, "That big guy with glasses told me to go home. He said I was sleeping." I said, "Were you sleeping?" He said, "No." This is a miserable place. I mean it's hot in the summertime. "No," he says. "He said I was sleeping." And I looked at him and I said, "If you weren't sleeping, you don't have to go home." Kip told the guys later, "If I'd had known what that guy was going to do, I would have gone home." So, the signal to shut down, I went up to the front end and switched the light switch up and down and went like this [NC motions with his arms]. Down they go, all of them. All the noise, everything stopped. And there were guys in there working putting pipes up. One of them came to me later on after we got back on – it only lasted 25 minutes, maybe an half an hour – and he says, "Man, I've worked at a lot of places and I have never seen things stop like this." And I said, "It's what you call cooperation." He found out what it was about. Well anyway, I started out the doorway to get the general foreman. And when he said, "What's going on in here, Neal?" Well I said, "What's going on is Jeff came through here and told that young man to go home. He's sitting over there now and I told him he didn't have to go home because he didn't do nothing wrong. He said he wasn't sleeping and you can guess who we'll believe." I said, "I don't believe Jeff James." I said, "He's assuming too much." The foreman said, "No Neal. I'll send him back. He started it, he'll finish it."

So, James came in and it was like a kangaroo court, everybody around him, ya know. And I said something to him. I said, "You don't have much use for veterans here, do you?" I said, "You know how I happen to know? Remember that nice plaque where people had all our [veterans'] names on it? I found that when I got back from the Navy, in a locker room by the urinals. So I didn't figure you thought too much of us, so what you did just now doesn't surprise me. You know the young fellow, he's a disabled veteran from the Korean War." He said, "I didn't know that." So I said, "Well, why don't you look into stuff like that when you hire people? You should know things like that. If you really want somebody that was sleeping, guess what? I was sitting down there while waiting for a run and I dozed off. Are you out slumming today? You're not visiting your high prized men in the tandem mill, so you slum and come to this dirty, rotten, stinking place and it's hot in here."

And I said, "Your damn right some people fall asleep and I'm one of them too. You could have sent me home. How would you have liked to do that?" Well he got the hell out of there. Never charged me with nothing. That was a wildcat strike. Never charged me with nothing. Know why? He'd have had three thousand jobs – the whole mill would have shut down 'cause that's what we would do, backing one another up. We ran it like this as long as I was there, and I left in 1982. We still had that. We were called the BJ department; that was our symbol. We were supposed to be the most militant place in Sparrows Point. I guess things just wouldn't be right.

We had a guy one time sent home. Now this was awful. This was a sit down job. I hated it. To be in that mill all night long… The superintendent got me on the phone: "What's going on?" And I say to him, "I don't know, you tell me what's going on." I said, "I hear people are all upset because we got a guy who was cut from the other mill" – and that wasn't my mill, it was part of our mill – "And he was cut and you people disciplined the man for being cut." I said, "That's all I can tell you. What can you tell me?" Well when you're absolutely wrong, you get disciplined. We each got two days off for that – everybody that took part in it. But I said I'd rather walk out than sit in there all night long without getting paid for it.

I got as far as alternative zone committeeman. See, politics in the union was rough stuff too, ya know. You ran against the guy and they're tearing one another up just like they do out here, what the Democrats are doing now. And I don't think… I couldn't go for that really. If you're my friend, I can't be ripping you up and later on say "it's just politics." And I liked what I did, too. Especially when I became the annealing operator – a nice responsible job and I liked it. So I didn't aspire to being, ya know… In fact, I was gonna work until I was 65 at least. I retired at 63 because of my wife's health back then. And I always felt it was the right thing to do. I was able to take care of her. She'd had a heart attack and then a stroke and she survived another 20 years. She didn't succumb to the heart troubles; she developed cancer, and that was it.

Well I don't think my kids liked to be quiet when I was working the midnight turn. I never could sleep right on midnight turns. But I guess they all pretty well accepted that that was what Pop does. Neither one did work at Sparrows Point, no. In fact, both of them joined the service early. One of them went into the Marines and just spent two years in. The other one went into the Navy, the younger one. I had a brother that was in lithography and he gave the younger one a chance at it. They both wound up in graphic arts, the older son too. The older son is very ill right now; he has lymphoma. He's almost 61 years old. The other boy's 56. But I have a nice family. I have four grandchildren, but I have five great-grandchildren now – one grandson and one great-grandson. The girls outnumber the boys. The one granddaughter is right up there near Rodgers Forge and the other son is in Ellicott City. In fact, he stays with me twice a week because it saves him a 55-mile run down to his job in Holabird Park in a printing outfit. He was laid off there for six months, but they called him back again. My biggest problem is keeping myself busy during the day since I lost my wife.

Well my retirement was a very abrupt thing because of my wife. It was a sudden, abrupt thing because I didn't want to do it to start with. But when I made up my mind, it was the right thing to do. Yeah, 46 years. But I always said I had time off for good behavior in the U.S. Navy. Well I would be up late after retirement. I figured the 12 to 8's working, I'd call down, just to talk to somebody because I felt an awful emptiness had happened to me. After a while I got over it. I was kept busy taking care of my wife until she recovered from everything. But I was gonna work a couple more years. The last year I made good dough, we finally got good dough. I think the last year I worked I made 35,40,000 bucks. I figured I get a couple more years like that, I'd get more pension. But I decided not to let the money stand in my way.

Oh yeah, 116-day strike. Well it was rough, ya know what I mean? It put you in a terrible financial situation. I was buying my house and I had a waterfront lot and I remember I needed some money – not a lot, about one thousand bucks. And I had to put both things up and mortgage it, which I was able to get paid off later on. And then you have to go down and picket, stuff like that, and try to get something to do. The Dundalk Florist, I worked there for a couple of months – a nice man who owned the place. I worked in the hot house I guess they called it. The morale during the strike was pretty good, it was really pretty good. That was over work practices. You see whatever US Steel did, all the other companies fell in line. They did it together, that's why it became a nationwide strike. It was bad like that but we won out on that. But you know what? They're losing all that now. They're losing it now because of the way things are. I can tell, a neighbor of mine, he works down there, he's about 50 years old.

Up until the time I left when they put that new unit in there, that high speed continuous annealing line, I kept my hand in that because I had a real good understanding of the rates. In fact when we went down there to meet with the industrial engineers and [Don] Kellner introduced me to them, he said, "Neal's going to run the show. Just listen to what he has to say. He knows what he's talking about." But they were hard people to deal with, Bethlehem Steel was. I left in '82 and I don't know how long we had the rate but I think quite a few years. But it was a rough row to hoe. I know we had two rates before we got one. What they would do is produce a time study and they wanted you to produce everything. In other words, if some orders ran two thousand, that's what they'd want you to do. You couldn't always do that. What it made you do is, it made you hold back. If they had just given us good rates to start with, it would have been better off in the long run, they would have got better production in the long run. A lot of deliberate things would go on whether you'd like to do them or not. A lot of the guys didn't like that either because you're putting the line down. But we finally got a decent rate. They've lost it since I left. The job was set up as a 4-man crew. And we said we needed another feeder helper back there. Finally we did get one. The guy that was superintendent one day came around and said to me, "Neal, what do you want first, the rate or the man?" And, without hesitation, I said "the man" because I knew that if we got the rate, we'd never get the man because the guys would start producing to get the money. We finally did get another man, but it took about a year and a half, just alone for that. Then, after that, was the work on the rate, but since then they've eliminated that. They've eliminated it with workers' acquiescing. But they were a hard company to deal with for rates. They were very hard, ya know. You had to con them.

When I retired, I had a sense that I lost something, ya know what I mean? Because here I had the authority over four other guys. I was the boss over them. I was an easy-going boss. I didn't give anybody a hard time. I had very few guys really test me. One made the mistake of doing it one time. Well, I had to tell him off, ya know what I mean? He come up to me like he's gonna, ya know… He was a young fellow on the line, and I told him he was slowing it down and letting too much of the junk go in, making it bad. The tail ends would get heavy, and you had to know what you were doing as an operator to slow that line down because that stuff would wreck on you. I told him, "Don't run that stuff down that way." I think this young kid was on something, smoking weed or something. So, he did it anyway. So, I walked back and said – and it put me in a position, here I'm a guy who represents people too, and here I got to chew this guy out – and I said, "Look, I told you not to run that stuff in. Now I'm not BS-ing you. I'll tell you what, I have never, ever gone to the foreman about anybody, yet I'm gonna make you number one if you don't listen. You got that straight?" And he just nodded his head. And he did alright after that. I didn't like to have to be that way, but I felt that I had to.

They tried to make a foreman out of me. They asked me to the dance so many times, they finally stopped. Every general foreman I would get would try to get me to be a foreman. I tried it one time for three months. Way back then, John F. Kennedy had called the heads of the steel industry a bunch of S-O-Bs. And man, the stock market hit the doldrums, ya know. So, they stopped using the hourly guys. I didn't say anything. I thought, "OK." But nobody had the decency to come up and say, "Well we can't use you now because of these reasons."This same general foreman who didn't have anything to say, he come up to me on the older line and said, "Neal, I wanna talk to you." I said, "OK. What did I do wrong now?" ya know kidding a little. He said, "Oh nothing. I just want to talk to you about filling back in again." I said, "No, Steve, I don't want to. Number one, I don't like the way you did it. This gives me an opportunity to tell you, you should have come up and said something about why you didn't want to be using us. I had to get it through the grapevine why you weren't using us anymore." But I said, "I made up my mind. I don't want the job." And I said, "You were in the Army in World War II, weren't you?" And he said, "Yeah." And I said, "I was in the Navy. I think in the Army you can go up to master sergeant and in the Navy, you can go up to chief petty officer. Steve, that's what I am here. I'm a chief. I don't want to go any higher, that's it. I don't want the responsibility."

I've always loved to read and I still do read. I read the newspaper every day, and sometimes I'll read other things too, maybe once in a while attack a book of some kind. I've always liked to read. A guy one time, I was working on some figures in the mill because my job then when it was running good, I could sit down. I was adding up a bunch of figures and he said, "You're pretty good at that, aren't you?" And I said, "Well, practice makes perfect." I don't think I was that great at it in school. The incentive rates – I made it my business to understand them, so when they presented a rate, I could tell if it was any good or not. I think I was the only guy in there that did, too. Nobody else understood the rates.

Yeah, I do remember that McCarthy era, yes, yes. It was kind of bad and scary stuff, ya know. I don't think it bothered most of the rank and file. Oh yes, I do. Not so bad in my mill but I knew one fellow in the union and he was a really nice guy too, as far as I could see. I think he just died not long ago. But they had messed him up in the union. He couldn't hold any positions in the union. He would talk to me about stuff and I think he would have liked to indoctrinate me, but I didn't go for that, ya know what I mean? I didn't take any of the bait he was putting out. I couldn't see the Communist Party myself, so I never was really interested in that. Those kinds of discussions were not really open in the mill. This is a guy I knew through the union and he would talk to me. He would give me materials to look at.

Yeah, I backed Kathleen Townsend one time when she ran for something. Yes. I went around door to door with her.

The last few years have been very bad for a lot of people. A terrible worry on them, losing the health benefits like that. And of course, these people under the pension system. Now they're not – mine's alright because it's been over 20 years now – but a lot of them have lost a lot of money in that Pension Guarantee Corporation. You know the supplemental stuff, like a guy might have left with $400 extra…sweetners, yeah that's right. There were no sweetners when I left, so mine's intact.

Well in my years of retirement my wife and I go places together, mostly Ocean City and things like that. And of course, when someone's health is not really great you deal with a lot of doctors' stuff.

Yes. The international stuff, the trade is really bad, ya know. I guess you can't buy any clothing anymore that doesn't come from China or Mexico or whatever.

If I had to do it over again, I would do different. I would never have worked in a steel mill. Oh yeah. Even though I feel that I've accomplished a lot in my life by working in there and making things better over all, it's a terrible way to work. And I'd say it's even worse back then than it is now. Working midnight turn is awful to me. Some people it didn't bother, but it did me. And you know they talk about your chronological clock, right? Well I think mine for sleep was messed up from working in the steel mills. I always kidded about my Navy service though, especially aboard ship. I said they'd had you so damned tired all the time, they run you ragged. I was in what was called the O division which was the gunners mate division. And so you work on the guns. Besides working during the day, you had to turn to and do watches. You were so damned tired, when you dropped into that sack you were gone. But midnight turn was always a battle for me. I would wake up every hour. It's a good thing I didn't have a tendency to be an alcoholic because finally at 7 o'clock at night, I'd drink a couple of beers and go to bed. It would help me go to sleep. I remember going in that mill and being so tired. I had to work that midnight turn—sometimes seven days of it at one time. And then we'd rotate shifts. Yeah, weird schedules. We had a four-week schedule deal. Sometimes you'd have seven 4 to 12's, then seven midnights, then seven daylights. But there was one week where you'd have all those shifts in one week. Yeah, you'd work two days of this, two days of that. You never get used to anything. I read an article one time that likened shift work to jet lag and I believe it myself, I really believe it. Because when I would go from midnight and go back to day light, I would have difficulty going back to sleep that night to get ready to go to work next morning. I don't miss that, but I still don't sleep any better.

I don't really know, honestly, what I would have done if I hadn't gone into the mill. Oh, I did start… My brother got me a job in lithography but it only lasted three weeks. I'm talking way back, in early '35 or '36. And it didn't work out, I got laid off. So, I might have been in that industry. You asked me what I would have done besides… I have no regrets. I figured I've led a worthwhile life and I've made a contribution and stuff. But like I say, if I had it to do over again, I would have picked a different vocation. When you're young, 17, you're not thinking of those things. And about my Navy service, I spent seven months in Atlantic convoy duty for the big invasion. It was after it happened. About a month after, we took big convoys… Then we left there, and they shipped us out to the Pacific, and we did convoying out there and anti-submarine stuff. People asked me, "Did you ever get one of those subs?" I said, "I don't think so, but I think we made a lot of Germans and Japanese apprehensive down there when we were dropping depth charges on top of them." I feel for them. Then after the war was ended, we were taking the troops up. That duty was just as dangerous then. We had to go through these former mine fields. They'd swept the channels, but storms would break them loose. Our B-29s had mined them and they'd break loose. We had to sink 17 of them. We had to spot them; if you didn't spot them, they'd get you. We were ahead of the troop transports. Better to blow up 200 people than a thousand.

When I came back to Bethlehem Steel after the war, oh God, well I got right back into things right off the bat. They wanted me back as a shop steward. There were some that never left, they got those deferments. And I think one fellow in particular had a hang-up about it. I put his mind at ease. I said, "Don't let it worry you. If they had given me a deferment I would have stayed too. You didn't do nothing wrong." He didn't run off to Canada, right? I got right back into the swing of things right off the bat.

Things had gotten bad during the war. There were a lot of people afraid of getting drafted so they're gonna do what the company said. They weren't like me – speak up, give 'em hell. But they let things go. I had one incident which was really bad, almost lost my life my first two weeks back there. These tanks would open up with counter weights hydraulically. You had to thread them up when a strip broke and there was a lever that went up or down. So, I was threading a tank with this guy and the crane operator is right above me in a cab. It was a woman crane operator. They took them all off. They were good enough during the war but they took them off when we came back. Discrimination against women, see. She kept ringing the bell, ringing the bell. So, in annoyance I went like this. [NC whips head around.] My God, the lid's coming down on us. It would have killed us both, and I jumped back and hit my assistant and drove him out of the way, and the lid closed. I went over to the office about that real fast and told them, "You better put a guard around that thing. It almost got me and Wordeski at the same time." And they did. I used to threaten them with safety and health.

I didn't know her, I mean the crane operator, from before. I thanked her. She saved our life. She must have been doing the heebie-jeebies in those seconds, wondering if we were gonna get killed. Steel mills are dangerous places to work, dangerous. There's so many stories to tell about them, ya know. I was only there a month and I was a crane hooker. They'd say, "Oh, a hooker." I'd say, "Nah, nah, not that kind of hooker." It was my job – they'd bring these transfer scrap boxes over and you had to get a C hook in each corner. And you had to get up when it was empty and jump in the box and grab both hooks and put them together. And if you're right handed, hold the hooks and signal with the other, "Take them away." Well the crane operator this day, he took me up, but I never signaled him. I had a hold of both hooks still and hadn't had a chance to put them together and signal. He took me up 80 feet. And the crane operators are good at what they do but he wasn't good at watching signals, I can tell you that. He got me almost to the cab of that crane before he saw me holding on for dear life, ya know. And he saw me and back down to the baler he puts me. I'm going over the shears cutting up the steel. And a cop come in the door. He turns me in in the office for fooling around. I wasn't fooling around. You had to be a screwball to do that. So the boss was a nice guy. I told him what happened; he believed me. He said, "You and the crane operator better get you signals straight." I said, "I thought I had them straight but he wasn't watching me." I'm not sure why a Sparrows Point cop had to get involved. I guess they used them in that manner back then.

I don't think the union is as strong today as it was when I was involved in it because of the downgrading of our steel mills because of the imports. The competitor factor is terrible and they've had to give up so much. I had a guy who was much younger than me. He retired a couple years ago. He said something to me one day. He met me in a chiropractor's. He said to me, "Things are bad. The union, these people in charge now, are giving the place away." And I said in defense of them, "I can't see how you can fault them. They can't help themselves. The companies have the hammer on them. The companies say, 'We can't have these work rules no more.' They gotta give in."

There is some people who don't know what the union got us. I think there is some of that going on. I've talked to younger people and they say, "Well unions had their place but they're not good no more." You can't tell an old guy like me that because I think unions have a place always. There's always going to be injustices. Somebody has to talk up and represent people; that's all there is to it. If all the people in charge were nice, benevolent people, it'd be OK, but they're not. It's human nature, they're not, ya know.

No, I never aspired to work fulltime for the union, not at all. But a lot of people did which was OK, but I didn't care to do that. I would tell young people today if they got an opportunity to join the union then to join them because I think people should be represented. I guess there's companies that have good relations with their employees. But my younger son, he was in the union but he lost out from there. Got laid off, ya know. But with this new outfit, they're non-union and the stuff he tells me – not good. But nobody's trying to organize them.

Mugs Rytter

April, 2006

My name is Margaret Rytter but everyone calls me Mugs. It's a childhood nickname. My cousin couldn't say Margaret and he got out Muggy, and eventually it's gone to Mugs. And it's been Mugs ever since.

I grew up in Dundalk, on the other side of the park, the second house, 3 Playfield, and safe as anything. You could walk through that park at midnight, people would say "Hi," you say "Hi." Go get a soda, really nice. We had little stores and the churches were all full. A lot of people went to church then. Pretty much everybody in the area was working at Bethlehem Steel or Western Electric. Yeah. I had a lot of the Lynches and the Todds and the Marrows all came in to school, so I went to school with a lot of them. I graduated with Morris Todd, whose father was a farmer. Dundalk was a farming  community. All the kids went over there, there was a ball diamond when I was a kid, the teams used to play, and we went right straight down to snake hole, swimming beach. It was a clear enough area, that was all. We lived on Playfield, which had two, four, six houses on it, so we all knew one another, and we all played together. Of course, the rest of them are Catholic, I was the only one Lutheran, and I remember Mr. McCartney lived next door to us, he would get out his fiddle and play *These Golden Slippers*. You could hear him all over the neighborhood, and a lot of nice people.

We had the Strand Movie, which is now a Dollar Store. We had a bakery right next to the Strand. We had an old five and ten next to them. Then we had a police station, fire department, and then I worked in the gift shop up there for fifteen years and they had a gift shop and a hobby shop and the restaurant, and it was just a nice community. Rundall ice cream around the corner, and then the third building was a restaurant and Duke's hardware store, he was there for a long time. And you don't remember any of that?

My father was a car inspector on the railroad at the Point. I had relatives down at Sparrows Point, my grandmother, grandfather and aunts and uncles, so every weekend we would get on the old 26 and ride down and spend the weekend with my grandmother, and she would have all the things I like to eat, and I knew a lot of the kids that I went to school with down there, because we only had eight grades over here. We had to go down to Sparrows Point. The town of Sparrows Point was settled. You could say that for it, the streets kind of would look empty unless it was time for mothers to be going to the grocery store or hanging their wash out, and I have a lot of friends still from high school. In fact, her walker, Goldie Lispecter -- did you see *The Dundalk Eagle* this week? Because her picture is in there, somebody wrote about her, so I'm using her walker, and we have been good friends ever since high school.

I started working, I guess, when I got out of high school, went up to Hutzlers and got a job. It's on Howard Street, and I worked in the wrapping department. Well, when I was a kid I used to get real sick on the streetcar by the time I hit Baltimore Avenue, but then as I was riding it every day to Hutzlers I could find somebody to talk to and it kind of eased it up, but it was scary riding a street car, because there are a lot of people you didn't know and not everybody was friendly, but Hutzlers was a nice place to work.

This was in '38, and when my dad didn't think $13 a week was enough, he got me on down at the Point, but I worked '40, '41 and up until September of '42. I flipped sheets of tin. Well, the tin made the cans. Some orders we would know what cans they were making and other orders we didn't, and we would pile them up and the director would come by and count them. He would pile them up and give them to the crane. Those women really worked, and we had Mrs. Alexander was our boss, very sturdy straight woman, lived over in Turner Station, but she really enjoyed having her job and always looked neat and precise, and she would tell you about your mistakes if you made any. We got a little lunch hour, about half hour lunch hour. Three o'clock, we were done.

I had to go down, put in an application. Cy Lovecan, did you ever hear of him? He worked down there in the office. He's the one that I went to, and he's also the one that filled my application when I quit.

I wouldn't know how many women worked in the tin room. I wouldn't know. Just seemed like everybody had like not a desk, but we had a place where they put the piles of tin. Another one there, another one there, there, and we weren't supposed to talk to anybody. The directors would get us in conversation once in a while. The sheets delivered by a crane to your table, yeah, they would load them down, and then we go sheet by sheet looking for the menders, and then they come back and count them and hoist them back up again. We just did that all day long? We got paid by the hour. We only went out to just the restroom, the lunchroom. Steps up to the lunchroom.

We had to wear gloves, but the tin would cut our gloves lots of times, but we could always get a new pair. Had to wear uniforms that wrapped around. The company provided those uniforms for us and you had to have it to be starched a little bit, and the gloves so that every day before I went to work, I had to put on a starched uniform.

We saw the girls at work, maybe on the street car going home, but we didn't mesh with them. There were quite a lot of them that were married. The ones that lived in Highlandtown were all married, and the ones that lived in Turner were all married, but we just didn't congregate except at the lunch hour, that's about the only time. We were all white. We call it White Turner's. No, there's on old part of Dundalk that divides to the highway. That side is all white, this side is all black. There was the street car bridge and a railroad bridge, but they tore them both down, I guess. It was so long ago, you kind of forget.

I rode to work with my dad because he dropped me off at the tin mill and then he would go over to the railroad. My dad he worked all 7:00 to 3:00. And then he picked me up on the way home, like on the street car, swinging and swaying. It was a nice old streetcar.

You go outside and wait for the street car or wait for somebody to pick you up and it was just vast, all over the place. You just knew there was something over there because they were building something there because there were buildings, just huge, look at it now.

The tin room was a separate building and almost all women, and then some men worked in the office there, and the directors were all men. I worked there from 1940 until September of '42. I was getting married. I was getting married on the 12th, so I left three days before that. My husband was a was a civil engineer at The Point. Neighbors of mine knew him because they all shot bows and arrows, and she thought we ought to meet, so she had us for a blind date, we kind of hit it off. He was from North Dakota, so he didn't know too many people.

He left North Dakota because they had a drought of seven years, and he rode the rails to Idaho, and he worked in the gold mines at Idaho. The only way in or out was snow shoes or skis, he said. Then he hoboed to Ohio. He drove a cab. Then his sister lived in Washington, and she was hired on with General Spatz of World War II to watch his children. So, she said there were opportunities for him to come there, and his brother, Henry, had already moved to Virginia, he was a carpenter. So, he came to Washington and went to a technical school, got a job down at the Point. He lived over in Dundalk at Mrs. Slimmy's on Baltimore Avenue. She had about three roomers, I think.

I seldom went back and don't remember anything about the union coming in in 1941. Other than going down to see my grandparents and going into the kindergarten once in a while and the movie, and I think Dr. Elder down there was the one that delivered me, and I just had a lot of friends down there so I would go spend weekends with him.

After I got married then I stopped work. I wanted a family, so we had three boys, and then ten years later we had two girls, and we lived in the apartments on Liberty Parkway, and we bought down at Yorkway and we bought down Waters Edge. My house is still at Waters Edge. My daughter and her husband have it now. So, I've never really been out of Dundalk except for vacations. I like Dundalk. The people. You can go to any store and buy anything, and everybody knew you. Walk in a drugstore and Cal Hunter, the pharmacist, "Hi, Mugs." Walk into Rundall, "Hi, Mugs." It was nice.

I never collected a pension or anything from down there but when Bob was -- I guess he was nine or ten--Mrs. Thomas and Mrs. Hackman in the gift shop on Dundalk, they asked me to come work for them. Of course, I had known them since I was a little kid. So, I went up to work for them 9:00 to 1:00 every day, and I enjoyed that too because a lot of people came in. Sold cards and gifts. It was a good town, and the hobby shop was right next door, and they moved over to Saint Helena, and I don't know what's up there now, a day care center or something. Cigarette store is what the gift shop is. I go to the laundromat on Mondays, and I go to Bible study down at St. Timothy's on Tuesday, and we have senior club down at my church on Wednesday, and Thursday I'm up to the Historical Society. I am blessed with very good friends that pick me up. because I'm past the time I could walk up there. I never drove, never had a drivers' license. I had five kids that towed me around and a husband.

I remember the old company store we used to go over there and buy stuff. It was a great big place, and they had the meat and the groceries, and they had something else over here you could get shoes upstairs, and my mother's cousin worked there so she always saw that I got waited on, and other than that I don't remember too much about it. My dad sometimes shopped there. My mom did, not him. I remember the B Street clubhouse and the drugstore was down on the corner, and there's another drug store further on down D Street and Eddie's Supermarket.

The town was segregated at that time D, E and F were all white. And over on H -- no, I, J and H were black, but they didn't come into the town itself proper too much, maybe for grocery shopping and they were likeable. It was hard to see the town torn down, especially at Bagan Beach, because we used to go down there and swim all the time. Yeah, things change. Look at Dundalk, all the little stores we used to have, nothing. Now people are coming back and buying houses. I wish my kids would come back, but they won't. They like big houses. I don't, never did.

Lee Douglas, Jr.
April 27, 2006

My father was on the railroad down at Bethlehem Steel, and, as a matter of fact it, was a sad situation for my father, because he was working on the railroad and then he went into the mill and he was forced to retire because of -- well, at that time they called it "clinker," a piece of clinker shot out of the furnace and struck him in the eye, and in hitting him in the eye, the foreman allowed him to sit on the side, and he said to the foreman that he wanted to go to the doctor and see about it. So the foreman told him that he didn't want him to go to the doctor. So my father didn't go to the doctor, and after about three or four days, the eye had swole up on him, and the foreman told him that "If you go to the doctor, we will run you away," that was the whole situation. "We will run you away from here," and my father never did do anything about that eye until it turned white. That eye, he went blind in that eye. Never got a quarter or anything because back then, my father was afraid that he would get fired if he go beyond the foreman, and that's the way it was at that time.

That was 1938, '39 and '40, and my father worked at Sparrows Point, and my mother and I were down in Columbia, South Carolina, and my mother and me, we didn't come to Baltimore until 1946. Columbia was nice. I went to school in Columbia. I had no problems in Columbia because my mother, she worked on the railroad in Columbia, South Carolina. I'm talking about during the war. In '40 and '41, discrimination was there, but you were taught to stay in your area, you know, and this kind of situation. Columbia is the capital of South Carolina, and everything is open, the theatres were segregated, you know, and jobs and all of that, but other than that, you got along. As a matter of fact, that's where I volunteered in the United Marines Corps from Columbia, South Carolina.

My dad was from Columbia, South Carolina, also. He came up to Baltimore right at the war time or right around the wartime, the Second World War. Until '39, and he worked in the mills to provide for us. Well, my father had a brother living at 1710 Madison Avenue in Baltimore, Maryland, and my father came up -- he told him to come up, and my father came up and went on the railroad first, and the railroad out there, rain, sleet or snow. So, my father decided to go in the mill. He worked in the mill, and when my father lost the one eye, his thoughts were getting away. All of this was instilled in me.

I got a lot of heartaches from the suffering that he did. We used to go through some tough stuff. I didn't really get involved until 1943. I volunteered in the United States Marine Corps in

1943, I had just finished going to heavy equipment school, and I volunteered in the Corps thinking that I would be able to use my education in heavy equipment in the National Youth Administration School down there.

When I went in the Marine Corps, I went to Camp Lejeune, North Carolina, which is located in Jacksonville, North Carolina. When I got in there, there was discrimination, segregation at Montford Point, North Carolina. The white marines were trained in Camp Lejeune, three miles away, and we went through a training at Montford Point. At that time, there were a few blacks that were drill instructors. We were not able to function collectively together because of the race situation.

The highest a black could be at Montford Point, North Carolina, in the black Marine base was five stripes. Anything other than that was white. There were no officers there. When I finished my training in 1944 and went overseas, we left Panama and went to Guadalcanal. As a matter of fact, as we were going overseas, we were on a ship with a little over 2,000 men. No food for the noon time. You get in the line in the morning and line at night, stayed in the line all day. The name of that ship will go down in the cemetery with me, the *USS Sea Perch*. It was sank on the way back from overseas and carried -- a lot went down. The *USS Sea Perch*, the boiler blew up on us in the Pacific Ocean, and we were left by ourselves, and I joined the church in the South Pacific, everybody joined the church who already joined the church before, this was 1944. We sat out there approximately four hours while they were working on the boiler, and then we saw the white foam and we knew the Lord was still with us.

We landed in Guadalcanal getting ready for an invasion though we didn't know at that time. The invasion was the D-Day, it was September the 15th, 1944. We was on Guadalcanal, we were training, we were snapping in, we didn't even understand why we were doing the vigorous training that we were doing, but we were getting ready to go to the invasion.

At that time, I was in the ammunition company, the 7th ammunition company, all black. We were -- we did everything. I was in the heavy equipment, road graders, bulldozers, and our job, or my job was once we landed, was to make ammunition fields. We had to clear the grounds and then ammunition comes off the ship, all kind of ammunition comes off the ship.

We lived in one end of the island, and we weren't around any whites because with all the ammunition we dealt with, we sent men to the ship. Sometimes I had to go, because we had -- if they didn't have a crane operator, I had to go to the ship, help to unload the ship, and then we brought all the ammunition back to the fields and stacked it up. The ammunition dump, which is what it was called, was approximately four blocks and managed by all blacks, that was my outfit, 7th Ammunition. We left Guadalcanal and went -- we arrived in Guadalcanal in June of '44, and we stayed there getting ready for the invasion of Heligoland Islands and the Peleliu group, and when we got there, they attached us. At that time, you could only be attached -- blacks could not belong to the First Marine Division. So, they attached us to the First Marine Division, and we went in the invasion of Peleliu Islands collectively together. We was supposed to go in D-Day, the first day. They assigned us -- the island, they did not look for the amount of death that was happening. They assigned us to the LOCI [Littoral Operations in a Contested Environment], little ship barges and we had the nets, we gathered up the bodies and put them in the nets, and then we brought them back and then the crane would bring them and they would put weights on them and sink them so that the ship propeller wouldn't cut them up. When we went in it was -- we were looking forward to taking the island in five to six days, and it was three weeks before because we did not know exactly the intensity that the Japanese were built in and boxes that they had. We thought we was the only ship September the 15th, D-Day, and we were watching the explosion and the ships bombing and bombing, and we just knew when we went in that everything would be dead, but it was a lot of difference, a lot of difference. We left after the Peleliu Islands invasion. We went back to the black situation, and we went to Saipan and we stayed on Saipan. We were there when the President Franklin D. Roosevelt passed, and I didn't even believe that we would come back to the states. I thought it was all over, but the Lord was still with us.

Roosevelt's death, it was a sad situation because we -- all our heart and hopes was into Roosevelt, and when he died, we did not see any means of us coming back to the states because things was so tough. Saipan was a large island and we had a lot of difficulty on Saipan. As a matter of fact, we in the Marine Corps, although this is not never told, I doubt if all the ones that know about it is probably in the cemetery, but we had a five-day race riot there at Saipan, and one of the sad parts about it was Bob Hope came over to Guadalcanal. We went to the theater that night. The theater was nothing but an open field. We went to the theater, black and white, and the colonel got up at the stage and stated that he did not know that the United States was at war until he saw the Negroes in his uniform, and we thought that was very objectionable words that he should use at that time, and we got up and we walked, all the blacks left and went on back to our area, and the next day we got word that the division was going to come in and do some shooting.

Well, we had the ammunition company and we didn't want anything to happen. However, we wasn't going to allow somebody to just come in and shoot, and this kind of situation is kept quiet today because the colonel shut the PX down, shut the whole island down with everything because he stated that we insulted him when the black troops got up and walked away, and it was expressed that we did not like the words that he said. He was really stating that we were nobody, and he closed the PX down, and the chaplain filed a complaint and made it -- opened it up again because he used the article that we were at divine services, and that in order to close something down, that would be the article that you had to use and he did that.

And my experience overseas has been a good one and a sad one. In my outfit, the first person that got killed in our outfit -- I can't even think of his name now, because 62 years ago his name is gone from me. He was from Philadelphia and he got blew up, and the next one, a 37-millimeter went through his body, but we were able to work collectively, black and white were able to work collectively together, although most of our time in the Marine Corps was separated. We had seen everything that you could see. We were looking forward to coming back to the United States. There was no black officers in the Marine Corps, all white. In my outfit, the highest a black could be was three stripes. If you got to a four, which is a platoon sergeant, then the white comes in, and this is the kind of situation, platoon sergeant and then Gunnery Sergeant.

Master Sergeant, we did not have. It was very difficult to make rank in the Marine Corps. When I was a corporal, I felt as if I was the king, you know.

I got along very bad with my commanding officer. He was from Greenville, South Carolina, God bless his soul, I know he's gone today because he was much older. His name was W.O. Livesey, and he was a segregationist from way back, and as a matter of fact, he was so bad on Guadalcanal he would give our equipment away -- whites would come -- we carried our own equipment because we was an ammunition company. Road graders, bulldozers, trucks and everything, and he would let them come and take our brand-new stuff when we come overseas and gave us old stuff, you know, just those things at the time. We, the blacks today, tries to sweep that under the rug because you move on, you know.

I'm probably the only one sometimes, when we go to Washington, I tell this, but they don't want me to tell it. They say "Brother Douglas, keep it nice," you know, but I look back at the persons and the fellows that died with me, and I look at the ones who die now in Iraq and it disturbs me from no end.

As of last October the 3rd, I was 80 years of age, and I am thankful to the Lord that he allows me to continue on. I was baptized in 1944. I did not really reach and grab the Lord's hand until '74, and today I am -- I have served in many capacities, including the reverend badge in my pocket, but I'm thankful to the Lord for what he's done in delivering me overseas and to fight for my country. If I had to do it again, I would do it all over again. If I had to choose the branch of service that I would go into, I would go in the United States Marines Corps, although things are much better today. They don't even know nothing, they don't have an idea of the stuff that we went through.

Back in Montford Point, you could be slapped, knocked down with the fist and punished and for nothing --I have seen people get hurt, maimed, and I have seen them get discharged out of the service for disability for what happened in the Marines Corps. When the first people got drowned way back in Parris Island, South Carolina, when the drill instructor gave an order for them to march out in the bay and didn't give the order to the rear, and they drowned, a lot of that started making the higher-ups in the Marines Corps take notice to things that were happening down below, because I never believed that a person could be treated like I was treated when I went in the Corps. And to this day I don't like it. It was unnecessary.

If you got mail, you had to go through the belt line, you get a whipping, if you got letters, you know. Sometimes things went too far, and I was one that rebelled all the way through the Marines Corps, things of that nature I felt was wrong. My captain, Captain Livesey, I was going in the office to tell him about them about transferring our equipment into the white areas, and he would tell me to get the hell out of his office, and as I would get ready to go out, he would say "What are you supposed to do," and I would turn around and salute him. He knew my feeling. He couldn't stand me and I couldn't stand him, and we existed, you know, but one other thing happened in one of the persons from Stark, Florida. We got ready, we are leaving Guadalcanal going to the invasion, and they was treating one man so bad, he told this officer, he said "When we get in the invasion, I'm going to kill you," and his name was Graham, I can't think of his first name now. They sent him back to the United States with a dishonorable discharge, and I wrote a letter in his behalf, but naturally it wouldn't go nowhere, but I did.

I was the kind of person that didn't believe that unjust action should go on and I don't believe it today. I fight injustices today. I got out of the Marine Corps and started working for Bethlehem Steel Company. We went down that morning of August 2nd, 1946. I got out of the Marines Corps in June of '46, and I had taken a mud hole and I went looking for a job and I went to Bethlehem and we got down there that morning. It was seven o'clock, and we laid around all day, all morning until one o'clock and they started hiring, and, thanks to the Lord, I was hired on the first day that I went down there.

In the employment office, there was no kind or signs of discrimination or nothing. You could go to the bathroom, you could drink out the water fountain, and then that evening after they hired me --I didn't have no funds. After they hired me, they sent me over in the hot strip mill, the 56 hot strip mill, and all you could do was labor. When I went in to the mill, there

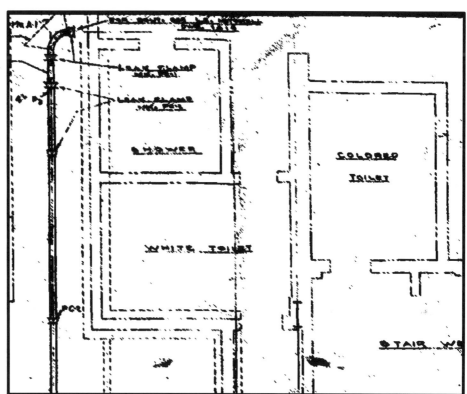
Map of a mill showing "white" and "colored" washrooms.

was a difference from the employment office. In the employment office everything was nice. When you get over in the locker room, outside it says "white," "colored," and when you go in, they had a colored side, which colored side was mostly always on the right and white on the left. It seemed -- I have always felt like if they are going to segregate, it seems the white would be on the right and the colored would be on the left. Or water fountains, you go in the mill – around the furnaces the water is -- you can go and drink it. As you get further down in the mill where the steel is rolling, high complexity, more money, millwrights and everything, living the life or furnace people, when you get down there, the water fountains is closed to you, but where they swept you could go and drink water at the water fountain, and I have always thought about that. A general foreman was named Stanley Johnson.

When I came out of the service, my dad had passed on, and my mother had passed on. My mother passed on right before I got out, and my dad passed on right after I got out. My father had glaucoma. I don't know where the glaucoma came from, but he had one eye and he had lost the other eye from Bethlehem Steel, and the glaucoma had taken over the other eye and he went blind. He lasted about a year after he went blind.

I was living at 414 Robert Street in Baltimore, West Baltimore between McCullough and Druid Hill Avenue. That's where I was living at that time, and my father lived on Sparrows Point when he was down there, but I was living with his sister. He had a sister and a brother in Baltimore, so I came to Baltimore and lived with his sister. His brother worked for Patapsco and Back Neck Railroad. As a matter of fact, he retired from -- he went into disability from Patapsco and Back Neck Railroad. My father had another brother that died from Patapsco and Back River Railroad, they were working on the railroad out there in the weather, worked on the steel side mostly all the time, and when I -- they only had one mill hot strip at that time. They only built the two mills. 56 was the mill at that time, and the only thing you could do is work in the labor department.

Chris Loucas

I became the first shop steward, black, in the hot strip mill in 1947. Chris Loucas was the president of the local at that time. He was a wonderful person. He was of the Greek nationality and he treated people right. He did the best he could do. I do not know where he was from, because the Greeks live somewhere around Highlandtown and Eastern Avenue, somewhere in there, but Chris Loucas was the president, I was the first elected shop steward in my mill, a black, the first black, and I was also the first elected assistant grievance committeeman.

What got me interested in the union is this stuff that I had taken in the Marine Corps, the unjust situation. And then at Bethlehem Steel, I'm looking at the same thing, all blacks working in the labor department. We've got steel running down approximately two blocks long. The steel that's traveling comes out of the furnace on a conveyor line and travels on down, and it's in a bar this thick and it comes all the way down, comes down and it is running a couple thousand feet. The thing that got me is the fact that if any of the workers down in the coil pit where the steel is going to curl up, if any workers stay out, they will call the labor department where I worked at and say "Send me someone down here to work today, send me someone down here tomorrow morning," and you go down there and you work with the whites all day long, you see, you are doing the bottom job down there, but you are down there, and then you can work down there 30 days, 60 days or a year, but you could not become a part of it, and it stayed in my craw.

People I worked with didn't talk about what it was like before the union because most of them was white, and whites didn't want to have a conversation like that at that time. That's the way the system was at that time. Baltimore City itself didn't remove segregated laws off their books until 1947, you see, and the first time that a black could go to the theater with a white was at the town theatre in 1951, because *The Roosevelt Story* came out. In order for *The Roosevelt*

Story to be shown in the theater, it had to be nonsegregated, and I even went to the town theater there on Frederick Street. So, things were just bad at that time, and in the union, they did not believe --whites didn't need a union. God bless them that they paid the dues, but they didn't need a union because they could get things done. It was the blacks that really they paid no attention to, and I don't know whether you call it -- I had been raised in the south and I hate segregation and discrimination, so therefore, I started working with the blacks that were being sent home for nothing. If they come in late, they sent them home, and unjust stuff I could not take, so I represented them, and I stopped all that foolishness, too, and that's the thing that made it so good.

My general foreman was an elder person and he didn't have much to do for blacks, but the fact he worked with them, so therefore, you could get along, and he and I got to be good buddies. He loved to go to the horse races. I could call him at his home, and if he's not there, I could tell his wife of a situation and I tell his wife of a situation that's going on at the mill—"They are denying this man the right to go down on the job and the job is not going to work him," and she would say "You tell them that my husband said let him go ahead," you see, and that's the kind of rapport that we built up. The big issues at that time was you did end it, but you didn't end it, but still you go down and do a job, but you could not become one of them

Charlie Parish, I know him well, he had an arbitration case in which the discrimination was raised for the first time in the steel industry. On the steel side. Yeah, he worked there, and he had about six or seven children at that time. I think he had about nine in all, but he had six or seven, and, as a matter of fact, I think I went to his last son's funeral about two years ago. Bernard Parish was a staff representative, and one of the things is that my doing helped Bernard Parish, it helped because they didn't believe in having black staff. We had a black staff man, I have a picture at home, the first black Vice-President of our union and he moved up to a staff representative. Joseph O'Neill is his name, and I'm there -- I have a picture with me in Los Angeles, California, with David McDonald [President of the Steelworkers, 1952-1965] with a hand on my shoulder. I was raising hell about -- this was 1952, '52 or '56, one, I can't remember which, we was at a convention, and I brought up on the floor, which they didn't have that coming on the floor, I brought up about the Sparrows Point segregation and discrimination, and he calmly talked to me about – I have a document over there that they put out from that, from the California convention.

Because that case follows through until 1950 when he finally got the job. He lost the arbitration, but there were two guys, a Stewart Huler Thompson– back then he was able to move up to the president of 2610 union. I knew all of them. And Mike Howard. And then GI Johnson. All these are 2610 people, because over in 2610, it was three quarters black. Steel side and blast furnaces and all that so therefore -- and then we have a member of our family that died representing the steel side, Rose is his name. Back to Charlie Parish, Charlie Parish was the only man that we could see working in the mechanical department, you know, and they didn't have a lot of people working in the mechanical department way back then. Charlie Parish was a fighter, Charlie Parish was a fighter, too, and he was somewhat like me. He wanted to raise his family to do the right thing, but you know, don't do me just because of the color of my skin, and that's the way he was. He reminded me of myself. We were friends for many years.

As a matter of fact, I started working with the 2610 way back. We formed a black organization, our side of the union called the Statesmen, and we would meet once a month at one of our houses. Well, the Statesmen club started in 1951, but it started from the tin side. You see it started from the BL department, which is the tin mill. There was a person in there, Floyd Rogers, and he didn't like what was going on over in the tin mill where he worked at, you see, and we started meeting outside -- all of us belonged to 2609 union, and we started meeting to see what we could do about some of the things. We would meet in one another's houses, and then we started raising funds, and we started meeting at the beautician club on Madison and Wilson Street. That was the way we generated, and then from there we started the Steelworkers and Shipyard Workers for Equality.

All this time, I'm, working as a laborer in the hot strip and I'm a union representative in there and we are respected by white and black, although they looked at me as -- the whites looked at me as a black representative, but I represented white and black. There were whites that wanted me to represent them in their grievances also, but there wasn't a lot of them because naturally a white person going to a black guy for representation in the hot strip at that time wasn't the best thing for him to do.

I worked daylight, evening and midnight. Nothing but just doing the labor jobs. If something happened down on the mill, you've got go down and clean it up, or if they need someone to come, we could go to any department. I've got a list of all the departments over there, we could go to any department and work, but we were just day labor, we go there and help them out that day. The people having trouble on the lines in the sheet mill, we go over there and help out. We would go down there and work with them in the pickler. We could not become a part of it, but we could get paid the same labor rate. Don't care where we worked at, that's just labor rate.

Well, one of the things about it, by me being in the Marines, the Marines Corps educated me to no end, and it gave you the feeling that if you did it, I can do it, and I will do the unexpected, and that was one of the things that the Marines Corps taught me--do the unexpected. Whatever they are thinking you will not do, do otherwise, and I was able to use it in the union. When I wanted to get something going with the union, I would meet not with the union, because when you meet with the union, you are under their laws, and when I was able to go and meet in Washington D.C., we did so without the union.

When I went to Bethlehem Steel in Pennsylvania, we picketed Bethlehem Steel. I carried five bus loads up there around 1967, and that was one tough situation. When we got there, we went and picketed Bethlehem, Pennsylvania. We shut the door down, the door that turned, that goes around. We were recognized after we got there because, as a whole, white people don't pay no attention to black people. That's the only time they pay attention is when you are disorderly. I had all these people out there, and we left Baltimore in May. When we got up there, the weather was changed, it was cold, and the women that we had with us, it was tearing up their jackets and their placards, the wind coming down from the mills there. I sent word up there to the general manager to do something, to meet with us, because we needed to come in, we needed the restroom, and they paid us no mind.

Now, the next word I sent up there that if you do not open up a facility for us to use the restroom, we will start urinating in your green grass, and in order to do that they barred us from crossing the street. When we got there, we couldn't cross the street. But we recognized that in order to get some action you are going to have to be disobedient, so I called a group of them together, I said "Listen, I've got to have at least 40 people that can go to jail and I'm going to be one of them. I've got to have those that don't have no five days penalties and all that, you can get five." These were all people working at Sparrows Point, and the women went with the men, and so I've got to have at least 40 people that can stand to go to jail without losing their job, and I was able to get them.

So, I said "Now what we're going to do we're going to cross over there where they've got their officers at saying they are going to lock us up if we cross over. We will cross over." We crossed over, and they didn't lock us up because the news media were there, and they didn't want to the news media to see them arresting their own people for trying to get just rights.

So, after we got over across the street where they barred us from, then I said, "That's not the key." I sent a message upstairs again that we want to meet. I said, "We have eleven people." They sent down and say, "We will probably, if you keep your discipline, we will meet with five." I said "We're not going to tell you how many people to have up there and don't you tell us, because our executive board consists of eleven people," and we squabbled, and I took a knock on one person and they met with us. But in order to do that, we had to get to -- we decided to go to jail again. We stopped the turn door from coming, we wouldn't let them come out. They couldn't come out. We stood there and held the door, and said "Well, lock us up." So, then they started meeting. They called us and let us know that we were going -- I went upstairs and I met with them and we laid our stuff out—we were the steelworkers and the shipyard workers.

This was workers of Bethlehem Steel, and this is the message that I sent up there-- all of us are employees of this company, you will not let us in to use your restrooms, but we have employees of the company, you see, and so then I said to them "We must defy. They don't pay no attention to people being nice." So, they told us that we have three people that need to get to out. I said "Look, let them out, let those people go." We held it again, and then they sent for us, told us to come on up. We went up and sat down, and when I laid out the things that we wanted --- we asked them for six things. We want to eliminate racial segregation. We want to eliminate the bull jive testing, because they tested who they wanted to test, and we wanted to be able to move throughout the plant with seniority, and they agreed to these things, but they didn't want to agree to them unionwise. They said "Listen, all we are going to tell you is that before you get back to Sparrows Point, these things will be in the making," and I got them over there that they was in the making, and several things that didn't come. Then I called the general manager and told the general manager that I need to have a few meetings with him, not with the union, so that we can iron out the situation.

The union officers were not sympathetic. Oh, no, because you see the union had to keep a response to the white workers. The white worker didn't need no union, but they were paying the dues, and the union had to still show that they were strong with the majority of the workers, which was white, and I could understand that, you know, but the factors are that we knew that we had -- here is where the trick came.

When we got ready to go to Washington, I had started meeting at 732 North Eden Street with the Congress of Racial Equality. I asked for a representative to come down, and they sent down Lincoln Lynch from New York City, and the idea that a top Congress of Racial Equality troublemaker would come in to Baltimore gave us a great help. We went to Washington D.C. and they were at the table with us and they did a very good job.

I had to break away from them though, because after we got things moving, they held a press conference without us, and they talked about them crackers down there denying blacks the right to go here and stuff. You see, they can go back to New York City and got no worry. We've got to go back down in the mill, so I fired them, and then I had smoothed all that out.

At the time, I was living in Turner Station. I moved in the city -- I moved back in the city in August of '57, but I was connected to Turner Station down in there and the situation with the shipyard. There was a man living on Main Street, and he was a preacher, Reverend Fleming, he was a member of the Steelworkers and Shipyard Workers for Equality. I said to Reverend Fleming, I said "Listen, I need the shipyard to come in with us, they are having the same problems we have, and he told me, he say "Make contact with Reverend [Oscar] Hoggs because he stands up for the people over there in the shipyard." So, I said "Well, that's good." I got in contact with Reverend Hoggs, and Reverend Hoggs met with me and three more of our officers, and we agreed to come together. This was 1965.

Rev. Oscar Hoggs(l) and Lee Douglass

Oh, yes. Oh, yes, the Civil Right Act helped us very well, because we were able to use that. Every time we would challenge the company, we had to use that. It was a blessing to us, and it was a Godsend. With the shipyard, all of their employment was similar, but they were looking forward to salary situation, and we hired -- didn't have to pay him but a dollar, but we hired Gerald Smith, an attorney-at-law, to advise me. He was with the NAACP education and he came with us and he advised us. His office was down there on St. Paul Street, and as a matter of fact his office is 727 St. Paul, right off of Madison Street, and he was a good advisor for us, because when I fired the Congress of Racial Equality, I discussed it with him because we had a meeting on Sparrows Point away from the main office. We hired a truck and put it there, and then the Congress of Racial Equality went in to that white stuff, that's the way they agitated the situation see, but the only thing about it they never recognized that we are the ones has to go back in the mill. When I went to the mill that next day, they jumped me, they said "Brother Douglas, all them names that you all are calling us," you know. I said "Now, it was from a group from New York City and we are not with them any more because we are not trying to alienate none of the situation that we are trying to do here."

There was a backlash with elections. I ran for election all the time. Bartee beat me. I ran the as first black -- well, the second black man that ever ran for vice-president on the ticket. They had two tickets all the time, like Democrat and Republican. First, I was with a ticket that they called the blue ticket. John O'Connor was the president, and the ticket that I was with was like a liberal ticket. Well, naturally they was against that ticket, whites was against the ticket. But we tricked them like the situation going on between the United States Senate seat, you know. I was a candidate and they were running a white person against me on the ticket. Well, they were smart enough to reach and get Bartee and they ran Bartee against me, so Bartee won, that other ticket won, because it was a Republican ticket, it was a conservative ticket you see.

Of course, when Bartee was a little boy, Bartee used to shine my shoes, I used to give Bartee money. Bartee used to come out and look after me, I was living on the Point and Bartee -- as a matter of fact, I would throw Bartee some money. Bartee is crazy about me. Bartee would do anything for me. Although we ran against one another, he was on the other ticket, and I didn't care, because I was known as a rebel riser, so Bartee was the man that got along with all whites. So naturally I lost, but it didn't bother me none because we were able to get a black man for the first time in years. So the core group was here around 1966 or '67? Oh, yes. We continued with that group in the shipyard, and let me tell you, the trouble came when we got the 30.9 million dollars [settlement in the Consent Decree]. After we received the 30.9 million dollars, which I didn't even care about that part of it. My main focus was on opening up the doors where the blacks could go anywhere, eliminate the testing and the bull crap that they had going on.

Well, after we eliminated that, then they paid the 30.9 million dollars. Then we had guys, one of them was my first vice-president, he said -- they had a bar down on North Avenue and in order to -- this bar that they dealt with they start bringing steelworkers in there and they start holding meetings to the money that they were getting, the six, eight, nine, that's not enough money, and they started this kind of thing. We were not after money in the beginning. A white person, God bless his soul, his name was Irving Auerbach. Irving Auerbach said to me, he said, "Brother Douglass, you take a look at this," and it was all about reparation. I wasn't going to think about no reparation because I was thinking about opening up the door. They took and started raising all this here saying that we wasn't doing nothing, and this kind of thing, they didn't get enough money and so on, so I decided to go get away from the whole business.

Francis Brown was involved in this. He was the leader of it, and so when Francis Brown started this foolishness, I said "Well, I have copies of what I was after to see that the doors open" and that's where I told Reverend Hoggs, I said "We're not going to deal with them, because we were Steelworkers and Shipyard Workers for Equality, not them." As a matter of fact, not one letter went away without me sending it. I wrote all the communications. I was in touch with three other areas. I was in touch with one in Virginia and one in Alabama, explaining to them the situation that we were going on, and we communicated. Anything down south was a tough issue for a man to take a stand. It's like why blacks are not -- black coalminers are only four or five percent, because you are dying in the ground, you understand what I am saying? You are already in the ground, you don't want nobody to put you in the ground, so you've got to be very careful what you say and do.

The first arbitration down in Birmingham was to get a black helper in the blast furnace moved up to be the motor inspector. Eventually an arbitrator gave the man the job but he ran into a whole lot of trouble after that. I used to communicate with them --I tried to deal with people, and then they had another company that I helped out, it's out of business now. When you are going down to Sparrows Point and you make that left turn, I can't even think of the name of that street, but it used to be a steel mill right before you get to the shopping center where -- where is that place that we eat at where we go to dinner? Cactus Willy. Before you get to Cactus Willy, there was a steel mill over on the left side going toward Cactus Willy. Yes. There's a steel mill over there that had the discrimination. Eastern Stainless was the name of it -- wait a minute now. Eastern Stainless had two places, and then they had one on Billiard Street, wasn't it, and then they had one of these places that I had a person that used to live next door to me worked in the mill department, but he couldn't get promoted nowhere and he became the chairman of that group in there, see, and we worked to help out there. That mill closed down. I don't know what brought that mill down to its feet.

Some of the politicians helped us. Now one of the things that was beneficial to me is that when working for Bethlehem Steel, I took a leave of absence from Bethlehem Steel, a modified leave of absence. I was required to work two days a week. I worked two days a week and then I worked for Baltimore City. I became a director under William Donald Schaeffer, who was the mayor at that time, and I was the first black man that had left Sparrows Point. The white man who left was Mimi DiPetro, but I was the first black man that left Sparrows Point and would later work for the city and still work for Bethlehem Steel. Once I started working for the city, I never went back to work fulltime at Sparrows Point. I worked a couple of days there and a couple of days for Schaffer.

Oh, yeah, Mimi DiPetro – he died you know, he died a few years back. He was a good city councilman, though, he could get things done. I didn't know him at Sparrows Point, but I dealt with him in the city, and then me and him were able to talk about Sparrows Point and all of that. Mayor Schaeffer appointed me in 1968, '69 I think it was. Oh, it was very busy. It was very busy, and you see I even -- I worked with all the politicians. I joined the greatest black political group in the city, and that was the East Baltimore Democratic Organization under Councilman Du Burns and Senator Bob Douglas and all. I was one of their officers and advisors for years with that organization. I served them 30 years, and as a matter of fact, I broke from them because I got angry with the way they were letting John Hopkins manipulate them, and I joined the Larry Young group. I ran on Larry Young ticket and won an elected position on his ticket, Larry Young, and then he got in that trouble. Yes, I'm in touch with him, but I'm not in favor of the senator that they have now, Verna Jones. She doesn't hook up to any --Yeah, she doesn't hook up to no -- she doesn't want to do the right thing. When a person wants to do the right thing, I'm with them, and I have worked with Larry Young a long time, and, as a matter of fact, Larry Young and I, we were like father and son, but I pulled away -- Larry got to the point whereby 50 percent of his helping was for those going up. The 50 percent coming down stayed down, and I break away from them kind of people. Any time you get to the point where you don't help all people, goodbye

I'm still in the city. I bought a new house when I was almost 80 years old. My wife is a money woman. She's the queen of the money. My wife is a person that believes in doing the right thing. Any man that's attached to my wife is going to do the right thing and will climb, because she is a person that believed that people should move up and do the right thing.

Lee Douglass—photo by Joe Giordano

I was working two days a week at Sparrows Point, but the momentum was gathering toward a Consent Decree. We would meet with the government over on Pulaski Highway at the Holiday Inn. Yeah, because he had Schultz, George Schultz was the Labor Secretary, and we would meet with -- George Schultz didn't meet with us much, he ducked us, but he let the black elected ones meet with us, which was a good thing. A man named [Arthur] Fletcher, he worked with us very well. The only difference is that we could not expose what he was doing, meaning that he would meet with us and do all he could, but he is sitting in a position under other people. So, I didn't go to the news media and say that Fletcher was making this move or making that move. As a matter of fact, I was negative. I would say that "He said that in three weeks he would be back in touch with us," and he would have did so and so and so on, and I would say "I called him and he's not returning my phone calls." I said this to the media "He's not returning my phone calls," and then that helped him to continue working with me. I couldn't show where he was doing so much because he wouldn't be there.

In the election, actually nobody in Baltimore really paid any attention to George Wallace. I mean they wanted things for themselves, but they weren't worrying about that -- George Wallace sort of represented the outside and our steelworkers wasn't that defamed. They were looking out for self, but they weren't trying to do none of that stuff George Wallace was after.

Well, you know back in that time [1948] the local supported Henry Wallace, that was the best thing for the local union to do. You see the local has to think about what's their point of view and the surroundings of the people who they must contend with, and they contend with Essex,

Dundalk--that area was one hundred percent Democrat, and you got to understand that kind of situation.

Right now, they are jumping. I don't know which way to go like the people in Ohio, but I think they learned a lesson and they learned in this last election, they had so much turmoil going on in Essex about property and all that stuff going on [SB 509 in 2000], and it made the people feel as if they wasn't being represented by the Democrats, and I think they sort of mingled, and they wish they had not because there's a mess. We wouldn't be in the mess we are in if we had a Democrat president, and we are just talking, you know.

We had a union election in 1969, right after Schaeffer appointed me. Leander Sims ran against Ed Plato. You know, Simms was a good guy. Ed Plato was a good guy. Ed Plato and I fought like cats and dogs, but Ed Plato could get things done from the tin mill. He is from the 42 mill, Ed Plato, and even his wife -- I could get things done at the union hall from his wife. She was the number one secretary at our union hall, Plato's wife was, although they had separated, but I still could get her to do things that today I wouldn't tell. But between Simms and Plato, Plato has been a direct person. He was chairman of the grievance committee for quite a number of years, and me and him couldn't stand one another, you see, but the factors are, if you are right, so be it. Plato wasn't really a segregationist, but Plato had to play the tune in his mill. Plato had a mill that went over there next to Bartee. In Plato's mill, they had to keep that stuff going, and that's what made Plato continue, but Plato and I understood one another because I'm from down south and I understand the situation.

I was in 2609. I started under [Chris] Loucas and John O'Connor and all of them guys. As a matter of fact, I was the man on the floor. At every meeting, Lee Douglass is on the floor, and I was -- oh, we don't want to hear that, you know, but that's understandable, you see. They knew that I meant well and my words to them were this, "Today it is the black worker and I guarantee you in years to come it will be the white worker, because the first thing they do is they knock off their weakest link." After they knock the weakest link, then off they go and get the others, just what we are suffering with right today with no health insurance, no death benefit. Can you imagine somebody, say myself, worked 40 years for a company and retire and they take away your death benefit? There are people walking around with a tank hooked on to them and they took their health benefit from them. And listen, I have the tape of the union hall about that -- about the meetings that was held. I videoed that myself. And if the day comes you want a copy, I will give you a copy. That's when we had Barbara Mikulski, [Paul] Sarbanes and all of them come down and spoke, and I was down there with my group.

After the Consent Decree, I was working for the city. You see the thing about it is this, my main purpose was taking care of the organization --yes, open up the door, promote in accordance with your seniority, institute plant seniority, eliminate this bull jive that you have been having for years, you set up a test only when you know you've got say people, you know, and this kind of thing. "Do the right thing," that's all I said. When I met with the general manager, that's what I said to him, "Do the right thing."

When we left Bethlehem, Pennsylvania, they say "I know you are going to have a few meetings with the general manager," I said "Yes," because I had said to them "Do not hook us up together with the union because I do not want to get in that squawk." I understand the contract, I wrote grievances -- as a matter of fact, the point you spoke about, the lady, I wrote the first grievance of the women, and that's a thing about --although it goes back to me again as a black person.

The first grievance, big grievance was wrote by two women. Two women who used to work in the barracks at Sparrows Point, I mean at the Point. The barracks belonged to Bethlehem Steel, belonged to Patapsco Company, and they worked them there for years and years and years with the men. They decided to get rid of them. They let them go for two years and leave them out there, and then they had to replace them. So, they put them in the tin mill, and this is a sad situation. They put them in the tin mill, and in the tin mill they put them in the janitor place. They did not want them in the there. They transferred them to the wire mill. When they got in the wire mill, they put them in the nail department, and the women in there was in charge, white women were in charge. They would take the black women, they would take their nails and get them in line, and they would find bad nails in them when they come back the next day. So, they laid off, they laid off the two black workers.

The grievance committeeman was Ducky Jones, God bless his soul, I think he's gone, Ducky Jones refused to do the grievance, and I understand why. If you take up the grievance for these black women, then you ain't going to be around, so Ducky and I, we talked. I said, "I will deal it for them." I wrote the grievances for them and won. I wrote the grievances for the two black women, took near a year and a half before we won it. My age doesn't – you got me with the two women, but it could be easily done because it was only two, and Bartee would know them. This is about 1962, '64, something along in there.

And you see, the thing about it is when the grievance was won, to this day the women didn't come over to me and say "Brother Douglass, I thank you for that grievance," and I didn't give a doggone, I didn't want them to, but it was just the fact that she had the grievance committee up there, buying the champagne and going on, you know what I mean, and I said "If they only knew." You are sitting and feeding with the ones that were making sure that you wouldn't get the job, and they got retroactive pay. But things like that never bother me as long as I do the right thing, and I believe I did the right thing. They came to me and said "Brother Douglas, I'm having trouble getting my grievances done, and I'm afraid if they do them it ain't going to be where it's going to be winnable." So, I said I'm going to talk to your grievance committeeman as a matter of custom and a matter of practice and I will do the grievances for you.

You see, one of the things is I treated management personnel as I wanted to be treated. They treated me as one of their own. They were glad that I wasn't down there, and I was glad to be away from there. So therefore, I would go down there and handle grievances. They would ask for me to come down on a discharge case and I would go down and represent them. We had the highest respect of management, and I'm proud of it, that even though I wasn't working there every day, I could go down there, and it was just everything. I split time working a couple days at Sparrows Point and a couple of days for Schaffer.

I worked with Don Kellner. Oh, yes, Don Kellner. Don Kellner is a good man. He's my buddy. Mention my name to him. Don Kellner -- I went through all of that with all of them because there was no union meeting that I wasn't there, and I would have myself six or seven people always setting there because we are ready to take the floor on an issue, and the issue had to be with discriminating, something they do even within the union, they always look for me to --because I didn't give a damn. I would do the right thing. If you are right, I'm with you. If you are wrong, goodbye, don't even -- go to somebody else.

Well, what made me retire is that when you work so long, there's nothing down there as things are changing and changing and changing, and my name -- I have many whites that respect me to the day. I mean, the workers that work in the mill, they respected me for fighting for the underdog, many of them. And when I go to the union hall, we have seating together, and when I go, they come and meet me, Brother Douglass, because I always treated them with the highest respect, although we were different.

There's a bullroast Sunday for retirees. I was supposed to send my money in, but I didn't send it because what generally happened, I want Bartee or some of them to send me the tickets and then I sit with them, sit with people, because I have been away so long, I don't know everybody like I used to. I guess I have to call Bartee. I got the tickets, they done send the tickets to me, but I held them up because I wanted to be with guys that I know.

Oh, yes. I worked during the '59 strike. I did janitor work during the '59 strike. As a matter of fact, see, because I saw what was happening in the mill because I worked every day during the '59 strike. There an agreement with the union that certain people would continue to work to keep the place up. The millwrights, you had to have the millwrights to keep turning the mills over, and then they had janitors there to help clean, and this kind of thing. During the strike, I worked, but I also worked with the union. I would be out at the union hall, had people out there, and I would be out with the union, but I worked -- but they understood me working.

Yes, I retired December 5th, 1985. The first day my wife --did we go off somewhere the first day after I retired, dear? After I retired --after that, I worked with the city. I am chairman of Old Town Council Aid in Baltimore City, an area that encompasses the Baltimore City Jail, the penitentiary, Dunbar High School, that area in there. I work with the community, I am chairman of the community for them, and I have been the chairman for about 18 years. I used to live in that area, and I still represent them. That was the area that I was representing when I was elected, and then I ran on Larry Young's ticket and won on his ticket, and that's the area I'm on now. The Lord has blessed me to have been able to function at Bethlehem Steel, Marines Corps, Baltimore City, because I'm still working with the city.

Yes, I would go to work at Bethlehem Steel, because if I had to do it all over again, I would hope that the conditions, segregation and stuff wouldn't be there. Like in the Marines Corps now, the guys don't have no -- I talked to black colonels and generals, they don't have no idea of what went down. I belonged to an organization called the Montford Point Marine Association and we meet every month and we have chapters in all 50 states, and we have a convention in July down at Montford Point. You go back every five years down to Montford Point, so we have a convention down there. All the old Marines come together, the ones who are left, not many, not many are like me.

To me it would have been a good thing for my children to work at The Point. I have a son that worked at the shipyard. He was -- some kind of work with the ship, and then he went in the Air Force and worked in the Air Force. He's an electronic engineer, but I have no regrets, none whatsoever, because I'm thankful to the Lord that He gave me the vision, and the main thing I'm thankful of that I never tell nobody, but I'm thankful that I didn't get fired from Sparrows Point. I have challenged them strongly, but I always studied to make sure that I wasn't out of bounds, you see. Because if they would have fired me, it would have been a pretty sad situation. I would like to give thanks to the officers that worked with me in the Steelworkers and Shipyard Workers for Equality and thank goodness our main officers was white. The organization was such that they worked with us and did a most wonderful job. Some of them are still around, not many. Francis Brown is one. Robert Dalton who is a senator, Robert Dalton, 2538 Cecil Avenue, he's one. He was elected senator. He was the only black that was able to be on leave from down there, me and him. I used to write his grievances for him. He was a shop steward down in his area, and him and -- our secretary for the steelworkers and shipyard workers, Benjamin Hammond, I used to write all those grievances for them. I used to sit up at nighttime and write their grievances so that they could win their cases.

The future is good. The only difference is that they have to -- they have got to work toward Democrats. It's sad that it's necessarily said, but the Democrats believe in women rights and they believe in human rights. Bush got in saying "them liberals" and they branded him, but I can tell you right now, there is no Democrat would have us in the mess that we are in now, that we will be in for years to come. It is a serious situation and believe me when I tell you many people hate Bush. I don't hate him because I pity him. The man, I believe, wants to do good, but everything he does with the advice that he takes backfires, and that's where I think the trouble is.

Well, you know, I am proud of the people that I worked with at Sparrows Point. I'm proud of the people that I worked with in the hot strip mill. They had whites in the mill that was prejudiced as far as jobs were concerned, they didn't want nobody to promote to their job, you know, and all. But for going out of their way to do harm to blacks, we didn't have that, we didn't have it, and that is the reason why it was necessary for me to deal with the Congress of Racial Equality when they had this news conference without our presence and talked all that stuff about whites and when they don't have to go down there in the mills. I stopped that in its tracks right there and told them "Thank you and goodbye."

I would like to give thanks to my wife. My wife is a queen. My wife cares about people and she will do anything she can --listen, my wife is a city retiree. My wife – guess what? I was able to hire my wife for the city. Now isn't that something? My wife worked and was able to retire from the city from me hiring her; isn't that something? Well, my wife is Rosa and I call her queen. Rosa Lee Douglas is my wife's name and I am proud of her. Schaffer, our former mayor and governor, and now he's the comptroller and he is trying to do a good job as he always. He doesn't know whether to lean to the left or the right, but that's his decision.

The pleasure is mine in dealing with you because I'm grateful for you inviting Bartee and I down to Dundalk Community College.

Joe Kotelchuck

March 7, 2006

Well, I originally lived in Brooklyn, New York. We came here during the war in 1943, and I ended up going to Baltimore Polytechnic Institute High School, and the counselor told me about Bethlehem Steel and there were apprenticeships opened. I went down in '47 when I graduated from Poly and they were hiring. They were just looking for warm bodies at the time, they were hiring everybody, and I got an apprenticeship as a machinist, but that's how I got to the Point.

My father had passed away when I was about a year old, and my brothers, couple of brothers and sisters, supported my mother and myself, and there was no work in New York to speak of and you had the war industry here in Baltimore, so my mother and my sister and myself came up here. We moved to what was called Perkins Projects, and it originally was built for poor people. Then it was turned over to the war workers, anybody that worked in the war industry got a place there. We lived, I think, it was Dallas Court at the time, around Pratt and Caroline in East Baltimore, and, like I say, when I graduated from Poly--I didn't go to college until later, I took courses in college, University of Maryland--I was looking for work, and I spoke to the counselor from Poly, and he said there was openings in Bethlehem Steel, and I went down there and took the test for hiring, and they wanted to hire me immediately except I had trouble with my eyes, so it took another few days to get clearance on that, and I got hired as an apprentice machinist.

Well, I couldn't believe it. They were paying at that time $1.09 an hour for laborers. That was unheard of, $43 and change a week, and I never heard -- never made that kind of money right out of high school. I worked summer jobs and I worked one time for the B & O Railroad. I think they paid 44 cents an hour, which I think was the minimum wage. I was really in awe of it, started on the midnight term.

Well, I lived -- like I say, I lived in Perkins Project at the time, and I either rode with what's called the Red Rocket, which was the 13th street car, the 26. We called it the Red Rocket. I went up to Highlandtown with the 10 bus and caught the 26-street car, or I eventually made friends with people down there and I got a ride in a car pool. The Red Rocket ran all day and all night. One of the places it went to was Sparrows Point. It went downtown. I had incidents where I was supposed to go into work on the late shift and fell asleep and I -- well, you couldn't overrun the run going to the Point, but coming back I would overrun it because I fell asleep, and the street car conductor didn't wake me up. I went downtown, wherever it went, and then I caught it back and missed the shift going back to sleep.

When I started, I was in the machine shop, and they started you off, they put you behind in the tool crib, and you were supposed to learn all the different tools that they would give out. People would come to the window of the tool crib, and they had brass checks and they would give you a brass check and they would say give me a one and a half-inch drill or give me a quarter-inch pipe tap and a wrench, and they asked you for the different things and they had all of the stuff.

The tool crib also had a grinder where they ground drills and bits and whatever was used in the machine shop, and then eventually they put you on a machine. They either would put you on a floor to work with somebody, but during your four years they moved you around the whole machine shop, and you ran a lathe and a shaper, planer. They were turning out either material for the mills like shafts or gears or whatever they needed to produce steel or broken work came into the machine shop, and we took it apart and made new -- replacement parts for it so they could produce steel. They made -- over at blooming mills they made what they called hot blooms, and eventually they pressed it down into either sheets or cut it up and used it for various material.

A bloom is a big slab of steel which they made into a certain temperature and they made each one different -- I don't know if you would call it -- not intensity, but they had some were stronger than others, some were tougher, certain tensile. We were in all what you call the roughing end, and like I say the blooming mills and the blast furnace, the coke ovens where they made coke, and they used that to make steel.

When I started, over 800 people worked in the machine shop, somewhere between 800 and 900 people worked three shifts in the machine shop, and while you are an apprentice, you worked partly on the midnight turn for maybe six months and then they put you on the daylight or 4:00 to 12:00 shift for six months, and you went around and around, but they were different.

Out in the mills, they put you on a shift and you worked the shift for either a week or a month or over in the open hearth they actually worked three different shifts a week, but in the machine shop you worked as an apprentice, you worked all the different shifts, and then when you got out of your apprenticeship, the desirable shift was daylight, then they would post notices for it and you would bid on it, and if you had the time and the ability, you could get on daylight.

Now there was a lot of people that they didn't like daylight, they liked the 4:00 to 12:00, they found it easier, it was less stressful, and then there was some that worked the midnight, they loved it. It was sort of you worked midnight all night and then -- I just say this because I think they cheated on their sleep, and then they went and did things during the day, maybe they fixed their car, got a haircut, went to the doctor, whatever got done, and they found that it was a lot easier working midnight. And daylight, when they said you worked daylight, I lived in northwest Baltimore, I got up at 5:30 in the morning so that I would be ready to go to work and be at work at a quarter after 7:00.

I got married in December of '49. When I got married, I think that's when I left Perkins Court. My mother remarried, and my sister moved to another house or an apartment, and my brothers -- like they both lived in New York and they helped us manage because my father was gone.

When I got married, we lived in an apartment on Collington Avenue for a year, and then we lived on Brookfield and Whitelock, which was a real nice area at the time. Now it's kind of on the rough side, and eventually we lived on a street called Willaren Avenue, which also was northwest Baltimore near Park Heights and Garrison, and it was a real nice neighborhood, predominantly Jewish neighborhood. That's where I lived with my wife and started a family when I lived on Brookfield and Whitelock.

Oh, yeah, I got -- we got a car and I would take my turn in the car pool. I was with something like three or four of the fellows and I drove one week out of the month. When I was in the machine shop, I was always union conscious from New York because that was predominantly union, everything was union. Of course, I joined the union, but I wanted to be a shop steward, and when I was an apprentice, I told a fellow, a man named Jim Boyle who was what they called the grievance committeeman at the time, zoneman, that I wanted to become a shop steward, and he advised me against it because he said "You're an apprentice, and they judge you every three or four months and they can always find something wrong." So, I stood away from union stuff except to maybe go to the meetings until I finished my apprenticeship. Then I became a shop steward and became moderately active. Later on, of course, I got more involved, and I sort of went up the ladder in the union positions.

I think the union actually started in 1942, and this fellow, Jim Boyle, this man, he was really strong in the sense that one time I heard the story -- I wasn't there at the time--they fired him, and when they fired him, the men wildcatted for three days, and then they took him back, and the union was very strong at the time. It wasn't until recently that they-- like I say when they had between 800 and 900 men in the machine shop.

I think counting everybody at Sparrows Point they had 30,000 people, and now I understand they have got about two.

Well, I really liked it. I had never seen anything like it, and with all of those people, and I found my co-workers very friendly, and I didn't really run into any type of problems, and when I said about the money, you said beside the money, well, the money was the big thing. It was funny--you made a dollar nine an hour to start with, and every six months, I think it was, you got upgraded, and when you finally came out of your time, I think the rate was about -- for a machinist $1.66 I think it was, and then we always said boy, if we could make -- at that time if we could make a hundred dollars we would be sitting on top of the world. Well, eventually we did make a hundred dollars and then you looked at another figure.

Segregation was a problem, I mean not limited to the machine shop. The union forced integration, but there was still a lot of people that were against it, and I remember when they put up a notice -- it was an unwritten law that in the machine shop that the black workers could only be riggers, crane operators, helpers -- well, not even helpers. One time they put up this notice that said "drill press operator wanted," and one of the black crane fellows put in for it, and they just took it down, and we went in to see about it, but they said "Well, they changed their mind," but they kept putting it up, putting it down, and then, finally, he stopped putting in for it and then they got a white worker.

The union president at the time was a fellow named John Klauzenberg, little guy out of electrical repair shop. He was a C-rate machinist. He was scraping babbitt bearings and that was rated as C rate. I thought he was good. He was an honest sincere type of guy, and I got along with him. Of course, later on in union politics, there was a falling out and he got knocked out of the office, and one of his best friends -- I'll think of his name, took his place. I think he was the vice-president and he was the black man and he was the first president, black president of the 2610. No, Bartee came later. This was -- I can't think of his name.

Well, they talked about the organizing campaign at organizers meetings. There was Phil Murray was the president of the international. I think he came from the coal miners, and as far as organizing, they went into some of these small areas to organize like up in Highlandtown there were different companies, and there was always a problem, but they had union organizers and they were pretty tough type of guys, and the people that worked for the international, they did organizing, too, and they sort of worked like day and night, and they sent them all over the place, and they had the conventions in Atlantic City, I remember that, and that was before gambling.

The period of '47, '48, '49 when I was a young guy, the political activities, the Taft-Hartley Act and stuff, did have an impact on the shop at all. That was really controversial, and -- yeah, it definitely had an impact. I remember at that time, I was one of the Henry Wallace supporters, and he was the third party, and there was a lot of stink about that, but the union still basically went Democrat. Well, I thought that Wallace was the best thing for the day, that he was for the workers and for the labor people, and he had been a Democrat --I think he was vice-president one time, and then he ran for president, and I thought he was the best man, but it just wasn't to be. There wasn't too many discussions in the shop, but there was a lot of discussions at the union hall, at the meetings they had controversy.

Well, when you became a steward, you had a certain amount of power. You went in to see the foreman when somebody thought something was wrong and you tried to get it straightened out, and later on when I became what they called the zone committeeman for zone -- let me see, zone six, the machine shop -- it covered the machine shop, blacksmith shop and car repair shop, and they had -- well, in those three shops, the blacksmith shop had about 200 people and the car repair shop had about 200. The blacksmith shop went down to nothing and they did away with it, and the car repair, I think, they eventually fit it in with the iron workers. The car repair built and assembled and disassembled railroad cars that were used in the plant. Well, the Back River railroad-- that was a different group. I'm trying to think of what year it was when I became Zoneman. I think roughly in the late 60's—I had been there for almost 20 years

The 1959 strike? Sure. That was 16 weeks, we were out 116 days. Well, the people backed the strike. Nobody thought it would go that long, and we had a lot of problems with it. We went through any savings that we had, the wife got a part-time job, which was really hard because one of the questions that they asked everybody was where does your husband work, and when she said Sparrows Point, they said "No, we're not going to hire you because as soon as they settle, he will go back and we will lose you," and it really was the truth, and then some guys got jobs on the outside. They didn't tell them they worked at Sparrows Point. Most of them said they did work at Sparrows Point and if you hired them, they would stay, but these companies never believed that. Yes, I was on one of the committees that gave out food to people and helped approve loans to pay the rent, so people didn't get dispossessed. It was a big operation.

The union hall under Klauzenberg was on Lombard Street, somewhere near Highland Avenue. It was a storefront place, and they had an office up at the top, and then we had our meeting there. We distributed food. They bought a lot of sacks of potatoes and canned goods, and they gave it out to people.

Well, I don't remember which strike it was, but there was one strike we went out for one day, Truman was the President. Truman said he wanted to see Bethlehem's books. As soon as he said he wanted to see the books, they settled the strike. It lasted one day.

Well, a strike always was over either wages, or one time it was over health benefits, and we were paying something like ten dollars and change a month for health benefits, and they arranged it that instead of getting a raise or anything like that, the company would pay the health benefit, but no raise. They were happy, very happy with it, because it was just another thing -- well, when you pay for health benefits, it was like they gave you a raise with one hand and took it back with the other, but this way you got it, you didn't pay tax on it, and whenever you had to go to the hospital or you needed pharmaceuticals, that was one of the best plans around. When they said what kind of coverage you have got, you always said Blue Cross Blue Shield, I work at Bethlehem Steel, and that was it.

Oh, yeah, over time workers moved. Some of them --the ones who lived in Dundalk, of course they didn't move, they were happy with Dundalk and ten minutes to work, but everybody else. There was some -- a lot of workers bought houses on North Point Road, and used houses sold for about $4,000 and new ones for $6,000 and $8,000, and there was a lot of guys that come back from the service who were getting -- either going through school under the GI bill or making loans through the government, getting a lower rate of interest.

No, I don't think it had any impact on the union. We heard stories like where they put in -- there was always a debate on piecework incentive, and some people believed in it and some people didn't believe in it. The union originally thought that you should be guaranteed your wages, and they believed in a fair day's work for a fair day's pay, but the company always wanted to put incentive in because that was a way of getting the worker to work harder or produce more, and it definitely worked, and I don't know what year it was, but the union took a 180-degree turn and tried to put everybody except the laborer on an incentive. Yeah. Well, the people who didn't have incentive and stood a chance to get incentive and make more money, they were definitely for it. We went to Washington, we had meetings. I don't remember the year, but I was the chairman of the grievance committee, and I went along on the meetings.

I don't know how much of an input the people like myself had. I went to contract negotiations, and on the one hand I really thought that I was part of the makeup for negotiating for wages and other stuff, but the first meeting I went to on in the negotiations I was thrilled to death. I got a letter, a telegram in the mail saying you are part of the steel negotiating committee, be in Pittsburgh at such and such a date. I went there and I thought "I'm on the committee, that's great." Do you know how many people were on the committee? 600. So then I realized that hey -- yeah, I put my two cents in, but the people up at the top did the big work like on money and holidays and vacations.

Lynn Williams, President of USWA (second from left) and Kotelchuck (right)

Dave McDonald was a president of the International at that time and later was --I.W. Abel, Dave McDonald and one that was out of Canada, Lynn Williams, he was a good guy. I had experience with Lynn Williams. Lynn Williams came down one time and he was going to speak at a meeting of laborer and management, and they were building a hotel downtown and they were trying to get union labor, but the builders fought them, and I.W. Abel put his two cents in, but it really didn't change anything.

Once when I was in the shop, I was talking to one of the men and he said they got a program at the University of Maryland called -- you got a certificate. It had to do with shops, it had to do with -- also there were nurses that went there to pick up credits. You had public speaking, you had writing, and you picked up 16 credits, and it allowed you to teach, because I ended up teaching labor courses, union courses, and I taught at Dundalk Community College and also taught at some labor halls. I once taught a labor course in South Baltimore for the sugar workers, Domino Sugar workers, and -- I'm trying to think of what the name that they called the course. We went downtown on Greene Street, University of Maryland downtown, and you took them in the evening, and it allowed you to get credits, and some of these credits were transferable if you had wanted to go during the day and then other ones -- and there was a certain requirement that you had to make –"industrial arts," that's what it was called, and we had all different types of people, from industry and also, like I say, nurses were taking courses there, but industrial arts is what it was called.

I don't really remember what year I started, but I was active in the union. I was either a grievance committeeman or chairman of the grievance committee, because I went up the ladder from what we called shop steward, grievance committeeman, or we called them zone men at the time. I became chairman of the grievance committee. Then I ran for election, and the first time I ran, I lost.

I think Ivory Dennis had won at the time, he won by three votes, and the next time I ran -- well, Casey Robinson was the president and Ivory Dennis came along and he won, and then the next time I beat Ivory Dennis, and I became president for two terms, and that was sort of -- I ran several times after that, but that was the end of the political career. I did become grievance man again for the shop and the car shop and the blacksmith shop. Yeah, I got defeated, and like they said, they are trying to tell you something. Well, one time it was the treasurer -- I'm trying to think what his name was. This is terrible. By the way, it just came to me that one of the presidents that beat me was a fellow named -- my treasurer Donald Ervin or Ervine.

Kotelchuck as President of Local 2610

If you had the backing of the district, you were pretty much in. Al Atallah was the district director that started and later was Ed Plato, and Ed Plato definitely controlled 2609, and 2610 backed him, too, so he became district director and Primo Padeletti was in there for a little while and then Dave Wilson came. I had backed Dave Wilson. In the beginning, the first time around Wilson wasn't running and I backed Plato, and then the next time around it was Wilson against Primo Padeletti, and I backed Dave Wilson. The elections were really something, and then there was a lot of small locals that contributed but you had to win either 2609 or 2610.

In our shop, when they ran for grievance committeeman, zone man, you pretty much -- if you were in the machine shop, you had the advantage. There was a fellow that ran from the car repair shop and then one time they had a small department called scale repair. Frank Rose ran against me and he really got beat, and yet years later he ran for president and he won that election.

I was around when the first union hall was built, and that was Baltimore contractors had got the bid, and they built the first union hall. I think 09 was first and 10 -- there was so many people that they needed another hall, and then they built 10.

Well, the blacks filed a claim of discrimination, which it definitely was, and they were trying to figure out who was discriminated against, and Bernie Parrish sort of handled that, and they paid -- I don't remember how much they paid, 7 or 12 -- I think it was $7 million they paid out, and Jim Harmon was put in to help distribute this money. There was a lot of -- some blacks said it wasn't enough and they wouldn't take the money, and other ones like Ivory Dennis said "Don't believe what's going to happen in the future, what's in your hand, take it," and he took it as one of the ones that took it. So, the majority took it and then others that still filed a further claim.

Well, we didn't have that many blacks working in the machine shop, just a hand full. Like I say, later on they did become drill press operators. There were some apprentice machinists who became machinists and toolmakers. There was a fellow I remember as rate setter, but there wasn't that many.

But, oh, yeah, it was a big issue in the local, a big fight on it like who should get what and how much they should get. That went on for a long time. Then finally between Bernie Parrish and Jim Harmon, who came on later working for the international -- I don't know who made the decision I guess between the union and the company what they were going to pay out, I knew Francis Brown. He was very active fighting for black issues. Yeah, he was active.

Did some of the white workers oppose this whole move? Not that I remember. They just wanted to be involved in the payout.

I don't know what the issues were at that time I became local president. There was always something in there about wages. It was funny, we always said you could close your eyes and if the fellow talked about wages and vacations and holiday pay, he was a young guy. If he talked about retirement and Blue Cross Blue Shield, he was a guy that was getting close to retirement and was thinking in terms of the future.

I thought that Bethlehem Steel and company would last forever. No, I didn't think they would be in trouble, and it was only later on, when we started having trouble where Bethlehem kept going in the hole, and what was happening in my mind was that the foreign steel was being subsidized. They were also paying the workers there for sickness and everything else, and with us, when Bethlehem put in at times as much as 300 million dollars toward these different benefits, they became more and more an obstacle to try to overcome.

Yeah, Bethlehem was top heavy, and I think that that went against them, but I don't think that that was -- though they were top heavy and they paid them, they got people in and they paid them good wages, and if they didn't work out, they let them go and they paid off their salary, but that wasn't what turned it around. I think it was the foreign companies were -- we could outproduce them, we could outwork them, and we just had too much overhead, at least that's what I thought. And now we are owned by a foreign company

Yeah. It's hard to believe, but we always jokingly said we fought the Japanese and they can one day come in and take over or the Arabs because they are the ones that have the money.

I wasn't happy, but when this other company took over -- of course they really took everything away from us. They took away your medical benefits, your pharmaceuticals, your pension, your insurance. Luckily the Government had a program to pick up your pension, so I still get a pension and Social Security. Of course, now I pay my own Blue Cross Blue Shield and my own pharmaceutical, so I can manage, but had they taken away the pension and the Government not picked it up, I and millions of others like myself would be in deep trouble.

I retired in August of '91, almost 15 years ago. I worked there 43 years. And after I was president of the local, I went right back to being a shop steward, because I think you only needed five votes to become a shop steward, and I always was active as a shop steward, and -- yeah, I stayed active. That's a long time to work at one place but, if you are going to work somewhere, why not work there? Sure, I thought it was a good place to work. As it turned out, a lot of people got asbestosis or I don't know if they call it red lung or black lung, but a lot of people got sick, and at the time before Peter Angelos picked up on the asbestosis, they had a company lawyer who said there was no industrial diseases. Of course, he was -- and later on he got let go and he just said -- they got on him because he never told the worker that they were dying of this disease. He said, "I was working for the company, I told the company line."

Well, they had safety issues in the machine shop. Asbestos was one of them, getting hurt on the job. I mean in the other places like the open hearth and the blast furnace and the coke ovens, they had polluted air, and you had to end up wearing a type of a mask, and in the blast furnace they wore these rubber -- real thick rubber-soled shoes to work on top of the furnace because the floors were so hot. But one person did get killed in the machine shop, but basically in the machine shop they got stitches and burns from hot chips and maybe lost a finger or something like that.

When I was president of the local, we went down, we got a call one time and we went down to the blast furnace, and in order to show us what it was like, we put on clothing to work in there and we sifted the -- it wasn't sand. It was some type of material and it was so hot, so strenuous. There were two, maybe three gangs. A gang worked for 15, 20 minutes, and then you quit, and then another gang came in and did the same thing and then they quit and then they went back. Sometimes they would call up -- they had what they called Article 13, Section

Mark Reutter, author of *Making Steel,* with Kotelchuck

3, if you thought that it was over and above the normal, you could invoke Article 13, Section 3, and the company would send a man down and the union would send either the president or the chairman of the grievance committee and they would take the man off the job and stop the job and try to settle the issue.

They could refuse it if they claimed it was unsafe, but if he was wrong, he stood a chance of getting penalized, a day off or something, and a lot of times it wasn't right. One time I got called, we were up on top of a shutdown blast furnace, and they wanted the welders to go into the shutdown blast furnace to do some welding, and they said that it was too hazardous. Later on, management, one of the top management people came and they said they are going to work this job overtime, and the overtime seemed to change some of those people's minds. Suddenly it wasn't that hazardous. They put a rope around the welder and tied the rope off somewhere up top so that if something happened and they fell, they were held by the safety harness and a rope.

One time Sparrows Point -- I talked to people that lived there and they had a setup there and it was letters, and the foreman and the management people that were like sitting on top, they had either A Street or B Street or something like that, and the regular workers had the rest of it, and normally you talked about company towns as being really terrible, but I understand the Bethlehem company town was pretty good. They had stores that sold company stuff and they had the best of everything. The only problem was a lot of times if people wanted -- needed some money, they would get these chips to buy stuff, sometimes they would buy with them. Sometimes they would use them, and they sold it to other fellows at a reduced rate, and when the check came, sometimes they got nothing in their check.

When I drove into work, the parking lot wasn't bad. I would say it was about two blocks to walk, had a nice big parking lot. Of course, my problem is that if I looked at the job, I would say well, what do you think of the job? Well, if I can get past getting up at 5:30 in the morning and driving from where I lived 25 miles one way, otherwise I liked the job. I liked the company work, the union work, and even though we had different disagreements, I found it was a good place to work.

I didn't run into that much trouble in 1957 about the HUAC hearings. They had some fights up at the union hall and some disagreements and name calling, and over at 2609 they let -- they fired some people, but it wasn't that much of it that I was involved in. They pointed the finger at different people, and they come to find out later that some of the people that were making allegations -- I can't remember the man's name, but he said -- well, it was a woman and a man, they were naming names of different people, and it came out later that they named people they couldn't possibly even know, they couldn't see or know as many people as they testified against.

I remember first was the Korean War and everybody was sort of gung-ho, you were either for it or you were un-American if you were against it. But the company put in for different workers. In fact, I was one of them where the company put in and said that they needed me, and I got a deferment and I never did go into the Korean War. They wanted to draft me, and I still remember dealing with the man on the draft board, his name was Simon. He was a florist in East Baltimore, and he basically said the company asked for a deferment he said. "We're going to take everybody except like half of one percent," and he said, "We're going to get you," but I guess the company had enough pull, I never did go. It was a general statement. He had lost a son in the second world war and I think he was bitter.

My wife was from East Baltimore, up around Patterson Park and I met her while I was working at the Point. Well, I didn't really work shift work. The only thing I was on the 4:00 to

12:00 shift for four years. She wasn't too happy with it and I definitely wasn't happy, though it was probably the easiest time I had. It was almost like, you got up late, you had your breakfast or your lunch and then you sort of waited for your rider to pick you up. You went to work and came back home, got home by midnight and had something, coffee or something to drink or eat, and you went to bed and went on, and then by the time you were off on the weekend, you basically, in my opinion, lost your friends. Luckily, I didn't stay on night turn too long. A four-year apprenticeship where I went to the different shifts, four years of 4:00 to 12:00, and then I went on daylight for the rest of the time. Half the time, I was at the union hall, half the time I worked at the company.

When I retired, I was still active in the -- it's a group called SOAR, Steelworkers Organization of Active Retirees. I was the secretary there. I was also secretary in something called Maryland Labor Education where I was the secretary there, and I was secretary in a few organizations, about four of them at one time. Well, Reverend Everett Miller ran things, and he was -- we sort of laugh and joke about it. At that time, they had a lot of people in the Maryland Labor Education Association and they were struggling for money. You paid a little dues. I think it was three bucks a month or something, and much later on, like now they are still busy, they are still active, but when they first started, they must have had 30 or more people would come to a meeting, and like I say didn't have any money. Now they have got half a dozen to a dozen people coming to meetings, and they do have money, so times have changed. But Reverend Miller, he was very versatile, and he put me through work -- he was head of something at Dundalk Community College, and there was another college that he was active in--McHenry Bible Institute. He taught courses there. He always said that he could teach any course whether he knew it or not. After three days reading up on it, he could teach you how to shoe horses.

Well, I taught grievance committee work. I once taught a parliamentary class. I taught blueprint reading. Let's see what else. Like I say, I taught grievance procedure, I taught it to the sugar workers. I held various classes. I also filled in for some of the people at Dundalk Community College when they wanted to go away on vacation or for a few days, I took over their class.

I knew Don Yost. Sure, he worked in the machine shop. He was a machinist, and later he was a -- I'm trying to think what you call them, like similar to apprentice instructor. Somebody came up with the idea that once you came out of your time as a machinist in the machine shop, they either put you on the lathe or a layout table or on the floor and you stood there, and when they worked weekends, which they had a skeleton crew for the weekend, a lot of times the person couldn't necessarily make keys or run big machines, so they decided that they are going to start retraining all the machinists that they can do either everything or at least a lot of things. Not cross-training but training you back for the work that you should have been able to do but you hadn't done in a long time. Yost was one of the instructors, and we had about four different people that came out of the machine shop and became head honchos at Dundalk Community College for mechanical studies.

We had Yost. We had -- let me see. Yeah, Dave Ledford is a good friend of mine. I taught some classes for him. I still remember when I went in and filled in for him in a class, and there was young people there from one of the outfits that sent the people there for training, and he introduced me and he said, "Joe has worked at the Point, he is retired now, but he worked at the Point 44 years," and one of the young guys raised his hand and he said, "My mother isn't even 44." So, they felt it was a long time and it was like ancient history.

Oh, yeah, Dave is still around, but he teaches, I understand, a class here and there. He taught welding, which I could never teach because I never welded, but he welded, and he also spends a good bit of his time, or at least he did, playing golf. He was a zone committeeman, grievance committeeman. He ended up taking my place. I got sick for a while and he took my place and then later he ran and became grievance committeeman.

I think the machine shop got sold over to Voerst-Alpine. Well, I don't think they have anymore, but originally a lot of the workers at Voerst-Alpine were retirees from the machine shop. We had a lot of battles on that. They were sending work to Voerst-Alpine. Sometimes they paid us a grievance settlement that they admitted they sent it out and we should have done it and we got certain monies, but most of the time they were sending that work out.

Subcontracting always was an issue, and as far as I was concerned it never really got settled. Well, the truck drivers were always complaining. There were guys in Langenfelter that had more seniority on the Point than the truck drivers, and also I remember one time we picketed the main office, and Dewey Parks was the grievance man for the electrical repair shop, and he said that "we can fix these motors that you are sending down the road, we can fix them cheaper than you can send it down the road." They didn't want to hear it, and they came and got the police and told us all to disband, and we wouldn't disband, so they ended up taking our pictures and they ended up arresting us all, not right then and there. They come out with summons and tell you that you had to appear in court at a certain time. I remember a State Trooper came here, gave me a summons, and for a while there you was on record as being arrested for trespassing. I'm retired fifteen years. I would say it was about 25 years ago.

Well, I didn't really think about retirement. I was going to work even longer, but I ended up back in '88, '89 had a heart attack, and I was in laying in the hospital and I was thinking what the hell am I working for? I'm not going to become rich. I've had enough, 44 years and so - I was 62. Let me see how old my boy was. Fifteen years ago, well he was 52, 42, 37. He was well out of the house, and my daughter was just a few years younger, and my younger son is about 12 years younger than her, so they were -- let me see, the youngest was about 25, yeah. I was looking forward to retirement.

Dave Ledford organized the retirement party for me, and they gave me a watch, and they had something -- I think it was one of the military halls, not the military hall, but –the VFW, one of those places out around in Dundalk, and they had a nice -- it was a nice tribute they gave me. Oh, no, I never got to the point -- with all those years of working, some people like you say they continued to get up, but I struggled to get up at 5:30 all my life. Many a time I went back to sleep and then going flying down the road, and I was either late or just made it. I function better after nine o'clock in the morning at the union hall.

I don't know what I could tell young workers at the Point. I'm not even sure what's going on down there right now. My understanding -- I still talk to men-- some of whose children work there, and like this one fellow has two sons working there, they are working overtime up the wazoo, and they are real happy with it. Of course, they are not hiring anybody anymore. I don't know what kind of battles they have got going on down there, but they are speculating what they are going to do because this company is talking about buying another company, and you sort of wonder why is this one making out and the others don't. Well, they don't have the same overhead, they don't pay any -- I don't know what the pension setup is. I think it's a 401K pension setup. They don't pay -- I think they pay something toward the medical. I don't know even how that works, and the pharmaceutical, I think they pay for the worker, they don't pay for his wife or kid.

Well, I think there are different eras. When the union first came in, the people were conscious of how the union really helped you, and later on all the younger people came in and didn't realize what the union did. It was an entirely different story. When I first started working there in '47, did people tell stories about what it was like before the union came in? There were stories about the foreman would come along and maybe somebody had screwed up a job or done something wrong, he would fire them on the spot and maybe take them back the next day or a few days later.

A lot of times they joke about you break for lunch or for supper and people would take a nap, and one time they had open house and they brought -- people brought their kids in, and the kids came around and they stood there like through lunch time and they went up the locker room, people were sleeping in the locker room, and this one kid said "Doesn't anybody work around here?

My kids never considered working at the Point. I got my son, my oldest son a job in the summer part days. They used to hire a lot of part-time work in the summer when people were on vacation, and we always laughed about it because he went to work in a labor gang in the blast furnace and it took him about three days to learn to sleep on the floor with something under his head. He also was making at that time -- he was going to college and he was making good money. They worked a day overtime and they shifted every week, and he stood there about three weeks, and then he went to work at this job that he had put in for at the summer camp. He liked to do that type of work. So, he said -- here he was making about a thousand bucks a week with the overtime and the shift work and he went to work at a summer job at camp. How could he do it? Well we said well, you've got to realize the kid is about 20 years old at the time. Here he is working shift work, he don't even know what day it is, what time it is. He goes to summer camp, he is all day light, it's sunshine, swimming and girls, what else do you want? He made something like $300 for the whole summer. Here he was making a thousand bucks a week, and the wife couldn't figure why he quit that job. He could have worked all summer and made about $3,000 or $4,000. Well, they weren't looking to do that type of work. They went on to other things.

Janet Kotelchuck shows Joe's bulletin board.

Edie Papadakis Butler
July, 2002

I don't know why a steelworker, as hard as we worked and how we neglect our families and everything, that put everything we have into our jobs, why we're not well-respected like a police officer or a fireman. Not that I don't love firemen or police, but we're just thought about as dirtballs, you know. We have no -- what do you call that, up in society, we're not held up in society as being worth anything, but yet we have value just like the fire department or the police department, and they get all the special treatment, they get certain days off. If they work so many days, they get a break. We don't get a break. The one time we get a break is when we fall over. That's the only time we get a break, and that's sad. We shouldn't have to fall over to get a break or wait for our vacations or stuff like that. We should be human beings, and yet we're not treated like human beings I don't feel in a steel mill. It's a different type of person down there. They want you like a robot, and we're not robots, we're full of life.

I grew up in Dundalk and was the third generation working at Sparrows Point. As a child, you heard steel stories, everybody made steel around our table. It was my dad and my mother, and then my brother went down there. My cousins went down there, my aunt was down there, my uncles were down there, and all my father's friends were all steelworkers, and they would all come, and that's all I would hear is about what the mill was doing. I knew about the mill before I even went down to the mill. Of course, I didn't know what it was all about, you know, until you go down there and experience it. You just hear about it, but you have no idea what it really is.

As a child, my impression was that it was a big scary place. Dangerous and hard work. My mother would just tell us how hard it was to flip that tin and all and to stay awake, you know, and watch, examine the steel as it was going up there, and it just seemed like you had to always be on the ball, you had to be sharp.

Courtesy of the Baltimore Sun—Chiaki Kawajiri

Yeah, my dad worked there first, and then my aunt was there and then my mother had went down there. After I was born, she got a job. My mother was, and my father I think, lived in the city at the time, and then when they got married, then they both lived down here in Dundalk. My father started in '47 after the union came in. He was over in World War II at that time in '41 and all them years, I think. Well, he was a cab driver when he come out of the service for a while, and then he worked at Martins and then he went down to the Point, and then when he would get laid off, he would just go anywhere to get a job. My mom was a tin flopper and they always worked different shifts so that there was somebody home. At that time, we lived on Sollers Point Road. Yeah, we always had my grandmother watching us. She watched all of the children. I guess they could have walked to work but I think they took the bus, and then drove and my father would drive as they got more income.

Even if the place sounded scary when I was a child, there was one reason I went to work there—money. Well, my husband worked for the city and he didn't make that much, and I wanted it better for my children and all of us, and my sister come in one day and said she had a good job for me. She had told me about the opening, that they were finally going to have women go in the mechanical, and that's what I loved, so I went down there.

Out of high school, I went down there for a keypunch job--I think it was like in March of '66 or something like that, and but they didn't really call me until, like I think, like June of '66 and I was married and pregnant and I didn't get the job, but then in '76, my sister told me about a mechanical job that was opened, a helper. So I went down there and got in that big line, and it was a big line All outside of the employment office down there at Sparrows Point. The line was large, people were coming out of the woodwork to get a job down there. They finally were opening up the doors to hire again. They didn't hire that often, but this was everybody come from all around, who heard about them taking people. So, I got in that line that morning, and I lucked out and got the job.

My sister was there before me. She has already got 30 years there. She went in, I think, '74. My dad, he got out of there in '71, and my mother, she only stayed there eight years and quit. She just couldn't take it. He had 24 years. I have more under my belt than he does. I'm not going to let him forget that. Well, he got injured, so he got a disability and got out of there.

My mother went on to do the key punching as a key puncher like we used to be at the beginning before I got the job. She went on to be a key puncher all the time with the Automobile Club of Maryland.

My sister also went there for the money. She was supporting a little baby and she needed -- I mean it was good money down there. That's all you heard is--if you worked hard, you would make good money, so you went where the money was, and close and convenient, and one thing we did know from watching my father, is you could be whatever you wanted to be down there.

That is one thing that Bethlehem gives you, you can be whoever you want to be. If you want to be an electrician, if you want to be a mechanic, if you want -- whatever, you just bid into the departments if you can pass the test. If not, then you've got to go up there to school and learn it all and then go back and try again.

It was very hard when I started down there. I don't think they will ever accept a woman down there, not in my profession, I really don't believe it. I mean it's sad, because I wanted them just to treat me as a human being. You know that's all I asked, but it's just always that conflict there. It's not been easy.

When I started, nobody worked with me for two days. I sat on the bench, and I thought "What can I say to these guys to really make them mad," and I said, "I am getting paid for just sitting here." They are out there sweating, working their rear ends off, and I'm just sitting there getting a nice pay, and I told them that and they got mad, and the one says, "Well then, you are coming with me," and then I got to start. It was one way of getting them.

My father was tickled. He come to watch me my first day, he was there. Yeah. He wanted to make sure I would be all right. His friends come with him to see me. They watched me through the doorway doing -- you know, doing bearing changing. Yeah, I will never forget it, I looked back and I saw my dad. I was so nervous, I was hoping I was doing everything right, you know, but I was real proud.

It was just something about the steel mill that gives you a proudness to say, "I work at Bethlehem Steel," you know. I don't know what it was. Maybe it was in my blood. After all, he worked there before I was born, so maybe it was in my blood.

The Mechanical Department was bull work back then. We didn't have the modern technology that we have today, so it was all pinch bars and mauling and burning and welding and all that, much harder than today. Today we think a lot with our minds more than do the physical -- the physical is still there, don't get me wrong, it's still very difficult, but it's not like it used to be. We have different means of helping us now.

In the Mechanical Department, we keep all of the machinery and all the operations functioning from hydraulics, everything moving in the middle, clamps holding everything in place and oils. If there ain't no oil in nothing, it ain't going to run, and then repairs. That's the biggest, is repairs. We are always repairing something, keeping it -- you know, patching it up, patching it up. It's really a maintenance function. It has to be there. Even though they don't want us there, it has to be there.

When I got hired, I had to take a test. Well, thank God, I was raised with four brothers and a father and that's all they did. My father used to have motors hanging off the monkey bar trees, you know what I mean, and I used to watch him out there and help him and he would say "Get me this wrench" and "Get me that wrench," and I used to put my baby dolls hair up with cotter pins. I knew what a cotter pin was. Everything that was on that paper, I knew from my dad. My dad would tell me, and I would go and fetch it for him.

Yeah, he was tickled, but I think the most exciting thing with me and my dad was when I got my real rate as a millwright, my real rate. See, my father never got it. My father went over there, but he never could pass those tests. He got it through his work, so many hours on the job that they would give it to you. But he couldn't go over there because he couldn't read and understand. It's not that he couldn't do the job, my father was a very good mechanic, but he just couldn't read and understand what they wanted. He had that problem. So when Roger Shackleford give all of us -- grandfathered us all a C rate, Kathy and the other girl [Barbara Elliott], they were happy that we were called millwrights, but I wasn't because I felt if the men had to go over there and take that test, I'm going -- I wanted to be like them, not a man, but be an equal like them, then I've got to go do the same thing they do, so I went over there. Of course, I failed it a couple of times, you have to keep going back until you get so many jobs. But when I got my first real C rate, I went out in the parking lot and I cried. I come home and told my dad on the telephone, and he cried just as much as I cried. We both cried to each other. That's how happy he was. I knew he would be very proud of me. Yeah, because I got something my dad didn't get that he always wanted to. It's just that he didn't have nobody to help him.

He only had a fourth-grade education down in Baltimore City. I don't want him to feel bad because he only went to a fourth grade. It's okay. He went to hard knocks school, that one is harder. I never knew my grandparents—my grandmother died at 25 years old.

When I started work, it was both the men and the supervisors who gave me a hard time, but I really truly believe I broke through to the men. The other level, I don't think they will ever be -- but I don't feel bad like I did because they think that way of the guys, too--we're nothing, so it doesn't matter if I'm not nothing anymore, because the guys ain't nothing either. We have no value. They are the ones that are valuable, the ones running the plant. We're not valuable, and that's sad because we want to -- one time they said we were going to get together and be a team, and I cried because I really believed that we would be a team and it would be a wonderful team for both sides to join together. But it just don't seem like it's working. It's that friction all the time, and it shouldn't be. When you work for a company, you should be happy. We should be happy going to work, not like oh, my God, what's going to happen today or who is going to be on me today. You shouldn't have that fear.

The men were helpful to me. Oh, yeah. Oh, my God, I wouldn't have got my break if it wasn't for men that believed in me and showed me everything, showed me -- there is tricks of the trade. You can get all these books that you want, and there are still little tricks of the trade that they taught me. They have taken their time, and with me some things I picked up fast, other things I didn't, because I do not see maintenance like a man does. I have already told them that. I see it in a woman's -- like I told the man the other day, our rolls down there, I don't see them as rolls like you all see them, steel rolls. I see them as a washing machine and the steel going through the old-time hand washing machines. But I understand it, but I can't understand it their way. I have to put it in the way I can understand it; you know what I mean? They don't understand when I talk to them.

That's another thing that's bad. If I had it to do over again, I would have got more education and then went down there. See, I'm not educated enough to keep up with them guys. The way they speak and their terminology and my terminology is two different kinds because of my schooling. Now my sister, she can keep up with them, she is more highly educated than I am. But I just keep telling them over and over until they finally realize what I am trying to tell them or else they will just tell me go away; you know what I mean, "Get lost, forget it, Edie," or if they see me coming, they go the other way.

For the first couple of days, I was scared to death. I heard that buggy going in and out and I heard about all the people that were killed down there, and I swear to God I just thought they were taking them out by the dozens, and all it was was a buggy, like a cart that takes the rolls back and forth, coming in and out with clean rolls, and I didn't know that. Well, it's like a cart on wheels with a cable, pulling it in and out of one area to the other area. Yeah, it's on like a rail and the cable pulls it, the wheels, and pulls it into where they grind the rolls in the grinder shop.

Yeah, everything was big, real big. I just never saw such big bolts in my life and mauls, oh, my God, it took everything I had to pick one up.

There was a lot of us working there, yeah, and then I watched it dwindle down to hardly nothing now.

When I started, I couldn't wait to get out of there. I was just petrified and nobody wanting to work with me. I couldn't wait to get out of there because I had to be tough, you know, I was a steelworker now. I couldn't show them that I was a girl, you know, and I left, and I would cry or I would run to the lady's room and cry or something, you know what I mean. I couldn't never let them see the tears, out of fear of them making fun of me. Yeah, I was one of the first women hired down there. There was three of us hired, me and Kathy and Barbara, all three of us, in 1976, but they split us up. I was with just the men.

My husband was no help. No, he told my he hoped I failed the test. He didn't want me going down there. Just stay home with the babies, but I wanted a better life and I wanted the children to have a better life, and I didn't want him to work all them doubles all the time. I didn't see him, and I figured if I worked and he worked, then we would at least see each other somewhere, get together.

I always knew about the union, but like, I said, I feel I'm not that educated to get up in front of people and speak. My vocabulary is very limited, and I really am kind of like my father, I can't read and comprehend, but if you show me, I will understand, but you have to tell it to me over and over until I can fully see the picture, because, like I said, I don't see it like you all see it. I do not see it in a man's eyes. I see it different. Everything they talk about I see it different, even though they don't know I am seeing it different. It's kind of hard to explain, and I never really talked to a girl to see if she sees it the same way as I do, but I know whenever I talk to them about maintenance, I tell them how I have learned, and they seem to pick it up faster learning it my way than the way of the men would learn it.

I started in the Hot Mill, but I really didn't stay there that long. I couldn't take the pressure. I wound up transferring to the Pipe Mill. I knew that they didn't want no women there in the Hot Mill, and when I went to the Pipe Mill, they seemed to -- there was a man named Smith that was in charge, and he seemed -- didn't care what you was, a girl, a boy, whatever. As long as you did the job, he didn't care what you was, and I was happier over there. I didn't love it over there. I loved it in the Hot Mill, but I was happier in the Pipe Mill. I loved the Hot Mill because that's where I was hired, it was my home. I didn't want to go -- didn't want to go to the Pipe Mill, and I didn't like that they didn't want me there either. That was making me determined that one day I would go back. I don't like that somebody don't -- didn't want me there. That ain't a good enough reason. If I couldn't do the job, yes, but just because I was a girl, no, that wasn't a good enough reason for me not to ever want to go back there.

I was in the Hot Mill on and off a couple of years, but we only worked like three months or four months and would get laid off. I would work and then be on the streets and then work, and then be on the streets, and that's how they did until when I would go. When I finally went back the third time, I couldn't take it, I wound up going to the Pipe Mill about '78. I got into the Hot Mill the second time, which it took me 16 years to get back in it for the second time. Because that's the first time they had openings for me to be able to bid back into the Hot Mill.

So, for the first few years it was pretty rough in terms of continued employment, steady employment, just because the industry was up and down. When we came back to the Pipe Mill, we got laid off, too, over there, but the other two girls followed me, because they said that they felt I was the strongest out of them three, and when I got scared and I went over there, they followed me. They didn't want no parts of the Hot Mill either. They knew -- you know, they figured I was the toughest one out of them and I had left, so they put up the white flag and left with me.

No, we all come back -- it took me 16 years to get back there. When the Pipe Mill went down in 1981, we were laid off, and then when I went back, I was like in that bull gang or whatever. I had to go wherever they sent me. Sometimes I was in the 42, sometimes I was in the 56, went over to the steel side, went wherever there was work. Then I went with the pipe fitters for a while, then I come back to mechanical. We just went wherever the work was.

Edie talks at a Women of Steel reunion in Dundalk.

When I finally got back and got a number in the Hot Mill. When I finally got a home, then I got involved in the union. Well, the man that was there, Jimmy Romano, he had it like a family over there with them guys, and I really loved that that he kept them all together. He was a zoneman, and he was really good with the people, you know, and I saw that, and then I would tell him "Let's have something." Since nobody acknowledged us, let us acknowledge each other, let us show honor to each other since nobody else is showing us honor, so that's when we started that Hot Mill retirement party up there. Even though when I worked over at the 56 they made me an honorary member. I wasn't -- I didn't have no number, but their wives loved me, and they made me an honorary member.

We had a retirement picnic for a couple of years because it was hard work. It's not easy to find everybody and work down there and then me taking care of everybody, and it seemed like that was really bad when my mother-in-law was sick and my mother was sick and everybody was getting sick on me, and I just couldn't think to keep this going, so I had to surrender and tell them we couldn't have it any more. I had to let both of them go. I had to let the 56 go and the 68.

The parties were wonderful. We had great times. Up there – at the union hall. 2609 gave it to us. Well, they let us pick what day, and they left it open for us, and we were going to have it every year at the same time. That way people would remember. Like you would say the first Sunday of March, and then we had the first Sunday of October for the 56. Well, it was real big at the beginning, and then it started like people didn't want to get involved. It was just so much happening down there that they just said heck with it.

See, when they were cutting back, the boys were feeling like they were cutting each other's throats, and it kind of -- when Jimmy got out, the family was gone, it wasn't a family any more. We got new people in there in the union and it just wasn't a family any more. Nobody trusted nobody. You didn't even trust another union member, so they didn't want to be involved. They would say "We're not going up there," which was sad. I mean it's okay. You know even if you don't like somebody, you've still got to honor them because somebody likes them out there, their mother-in-law, somebody loves them out there.

I only did volunteer work for the union. Whenever they needed me, I told them, "24 hours there's the phone."

The current situation, it's just got everybody nuts. We don't know what we're doing. We don't know if we've got a job or we don't have a job, should we be looking for another job or shouldn't we be looking for another job, we don't know. The mood's not good. I try to keep them laughing if I can. Then sometimes they get mad at me.

For my father, well, they are just worried about the money, you know. I mean after all that's --they are surviving off of Bethlehem's Steel medical and the little bit of pension that he gets. If that goes, then I don't know what will happen. I couldn't help them because I'm a Bethlehem employee, too, so when it goes, I ain't going to have anything. I'm going to be out there where, you know, maybe it's sad that the whole family works down there because there would be somebody over here strong in some other area that we all can go to, you know what I mean?

Now I couldn't help them if I wanted to, unless I luck out and find another job somewhere. The only thing I'm worried about is my age now. I'm 54 and who wants a 54-year-old; you know what I mean? I ain't 26 any more like I was when I went down at Bethlehem.

I try to forget the bad times; try to only think of the good. I try to make every day good, you know. I don't know. I can't really say one special day, except when we signed that agreement [the Partnership Agreement] that we were going to be a team. I really thought everything was over and that we really were going to be a team with each other. That was about the happiest day of my life is when I signed that big paper they had down there on the hot mill office. Yeah. We all signed that, and that was the happiest day of my life. I really believed it, I wanted to believe it with all my heart that we had become one and that we would look out for each other. It's not good to have a separation where you work.

Other union people tell us, they keep us informed, or if one of the boys goes to a union meeting, they bring the information back to us and tell us what's happening. I used to go to union meetings, but I don't any more. I haven't really been involved in anything ever since I told you about the split between us, my husband and I. I just don't get involved in anything anymore. I got a divorce and my whole world changed. And when I heal, I will get back into it again. It's going to take a lot of healing.

At work, we don't have the parts. We have to wait to get parts to do our job, and then you have to patch it up and use whatever you can find laying around, and then they won't --

like I keep telling them to put us at a table and talk with us because our people have very good ideas of how them to save money, but nobody seems to want to hear what we have to say-- in my 26 years, I saw a lot of waste. I don't know. To me, they don't run it like other companies I had worked for. When I got laid off, I've had to go to other companies and work, and it's just not run the same way. That steel mill is run different than these other companies that are around. I worked at Glidden Paint and I worked at Armco Steel. Well, their supervision, when you were hired to do a job, you did the job and you were out at their gates. Down there, nobody is accountable for nothing, they are not accountable, the white hats, and we're not accountable, and so what kind of place are we running?

Edie with her daughter and granddaughter

Would I do it again? I say no, but I really did enjoy going to work, I really did. You can ask my whole family. They knew that I couldn't wait to go to work. Believe it or not, Bethlehem was my out of what I do around here, it was something different, and what I give this a hundred percent, I wanted to give them a hundred percent, too, or more because they always seemed to need more than what my family needed.

Now, my brother, Joe, he went down there first. He is retired. Then he married the other girl mechanic, Kathy, and she's got a disability and she's retired. Then my sister, Dee, she's retired. She married Mr. David Wilson, and he is retired. So, there's four retirees there plus my father, that's five retirees. And then you have my brother Gene, but he passed away, but he was out on like a disability because he had cancer, and then his son worked there. No, he left, and then my sister's son worked there, Dee Wilson's son, but then he left, and then it would be my brother Johnny and now he was 62 and old enough to retire. Now I'm the last of the Mohicans down there, hoping to make it through.

When we got together with our families, when we get together now –we talk steel. All we do is talk steel, how to make it better, how to do this, how to do that, try to come up with answers, how to make the union better, how to make everything better, always trying to make something better. But like my sister said if I don't get involved I can't make it better, I have to be involved in it, but I'm the type of person I've got to feel it in my heart, and I just ain't there right now, you know, it's just too much for me to handle. It's not in my heart to do the volunteering and work, and it ain't in my heart to get involved in anything. I just put so much of me into things that it's a disaster when things happen because I put too much in it. I always wanted to be normal like everybody else and be able to throw it all over my shoulder, but I just -- I take stuff too, too serious, I guess.

Well, I just have a lot of pictures of the people and my certificates that I got my rate and pictures and my schooling papers. I was on an industrial maintenance brochure one time, and I got the history that Mr. Cary Gordon made up for us. He made a little book up and give it to all the tour people, which I thought was an excellent idea. I think they should continue and still give it to people when they come through our mill. It's really nice, not just for a tour, but when everybody comes through our mill, because people want to know about our mill, they want to know what's happening. And I've got videos of the old mill, the way the hot mill used to be. I got the new mill, and then I got some safety videos. They were given to me from people. People give them to me, donated them to me when I had the club. They were videos that people made themselves. Well, it shows the old hot mill. It's really neat. To me -- I have been there 26 years and it is still fascinating. I just sit on the bench and look at the steel, and I can't believe it, can't believe that it will come out of that furnace down there, went through the reverse and rubber, then number five stand. It's just amazing, unbelievable.

I just can't never see a steel industry not being in here, but I just think that we should find other ways of using our steel. There's got to be something we can think of that we can use our steel for, or at least get some companies down there to come on our property and use our steel to do -- build whatever they are going to build. You know what I mean? That way we can sell it even more if we could get somebody down there to make a plant and use our steel. You know what I mean? It would be good if we could be a supplier to little companies around us. I don't know. I just hope we come up with something.

My son tried to work down there. He put in an application, but they never called him. Now he did get a job at the shipyard. He worked at our shipyard down there. He was a welder down there, but they kept laying him off, and he had a little baby, so he wound up getting another job and he went to another company. Oh, yeah, I wanted him there. I was proud. I knew he would be good. I like what my son -- I used to watch him. He fascinated me, and I think he would have been good for Bethlehem, but they didn't give him that chance, but that's all right. Maybe it wasn't meant to be. It's okay.

It's been an experience. I would do it again, but I would want that education, I would definitely want that education, and then I would be heard and respected where I don't feel that they hear me or respect me because I'm not that highly educated. I don't know the right words to come back with them except mill talk, and you can't get no points across using that, even down in the mill. You should have the proper words and then they would listen.

Eddie Bartee, Sr.
July, 2002

Things are so good as far as the struggle is concerned. You know you've got -- I don't know the rate scales now like I used to, but you've got some guys that are making $30, $28, $30 -- $25, $30 an hour. When I started at Sparrows Point, I started out making a dollar an hour. It was like I said when we talked earlier, it was like probably 7-8,000 people within my local, probably close to 11,000 -- no, 14,000, 15,000 people working on Sparrows Point at the time, might be more.

I started in '55. I worked a summer or two before when I was in high school. Yes, I was raised up in -- I was born in Baltimore City. I was born at John Hopkins, but my parents brought me to Sparrows Point when I was about a year and a half old. We lived there until -- when my father died, he was a steelworker.

I stayed at Sparrows Point until 1954, when I got married and moved to a place called Turner Station right across from the water. And my wife's grandmother, we lived with her, and then I put an application in and I got a house in Sparrows Point in 1957, and I stayed there until 1974 when they eventually decided to eliminate the residential area of Sparrows Point. That's when I moved. It was a blessing in disguise, because we would probably still have been there now because it was an ideal community. In those days, people didn't lock their doors. As a matter of fact, I just came from Penland, Pennsylvania. My brother-in-law had his car in the garage and a car on the patio and a truck, the keys were in all three vehicles, and I said "You are crazy." The garage door was up. He's got *beaucoup* tools and stuff, and he says, "Man, we don't have no problem." He said, "This is Penland." He made fun of me. My mother-in-law is from Baltimore, lives here also. He graduated from Morgan, and my mind went back to Sparrows Point when we used to leave our doors unlocked, go visit neighbors, leave Sparrows Point, come to Baltimore City. Nobody locked their doors, you know, and nobody bothered your property.

It was an ideal community to grow up in. It was a friendly, warm country-style neighborhood. My father died when I was 16 years old and we had eight sisters and brothers, eight of us all total living, and the people came in and just literally took over my mother's house. They washed, they scrubbed, they cleaned, they cooked, they took up donations in the community. My mother didn't have to do anything. I remember my mother getting sick one time and a couple ladies in the community came in, helped my father iron her clothes and stuff like that. It was an ideal community.

You had two churches, the Methodist Church and the Baptist Church. Most of the people attended either/or. You know, a few people naturally didn't go to church, but everybody knew everybody. When you walked down the street, you spoke "How are you, Mr. So and So." You knew everybody, and that's the way it was up until the middle 60's.

The middle 60's, that's when the civil rights thing, there was protest filed against the company with the EEOC saying that Bethlehem Steel discriminated, and they did, there was no question about it. Out of that came -- well, at that particular time they didn't have any black fireman, any black policeman. All the black people, black community lived on two streets, I and J Street. You had a handful, and I mean just a handful of black foremen. They had a few what they called labor leaders, you know. This guy would be like in the labor gang and he would be in charge of the crew. He reported to his boss, he would do what the boss said, and they would give him a couple of jobs and more than they did the guys that were doing the work. The foreman was probably making 16, 17, something in that ballpark, but those were the things that we were protesting.

There was a lot of jobs that blacks weren't allowed to do or that the unions weren't allowed to promote on. Your mechanical department, your maintenance period, mechanical, electrical, that's your machine shops and all that. It was just a black --very few, if any. And as a result, by 1968, after going to Washington and bringing the government in, the company and the union got together, and we opened up the plan that you promote with your plant seniority instead of unit seniority. They had three kinds of seniority. You had unit, department and plant, and, of course, company seniority. Company seniority didn't mean that much to us at Sparrows Point, but needless to say, they didn't eliminate unit seniority, but they said for now on we're going to promote by unit seniority, which meant that a lot of the blacks that were in those dead-end jobs were able to bid and -- they were money-making units, they were better paying jobs, and once they got in there, they could use the seniority, the plant seniority to promote, and in some cases they promoted ahead of some of the white employees.

A hand full of black employees, they opened the door a little bit in 1964, '65 for blacks to come in to better paying jobs, but it wasn't a wholesale thing. They had tests and all that kind of stuff that you had to take. I know we were working with a group of guys, it was in the sewing room where I worked. I did stocking, hooking, assembling units. I never worked up to a track operator. I never got enough seniority. But in the sewing room, we all started getting laid off. I had worked like six years and never had gotten laid off, and, all at once, they started downsizing the sewing room, and we got laid off, and this happened to me like two years in a row, three years in a row, and they had the unit that produced the tandem department. They had young white boys working who had less seniority than me with the company, they were working, I was in the street, so we started studying, a bunch of us, on our breaks. We had two breaks. Let's say you worked the 3:00 to 11:00, you got a break at five o'clock, and you get another one at eight o'clock. Well, during those breaks we had math books, spelling books and reading books and all that sort of stuff. Most of us had finished high school, but some of us was a little rusty, you know some of it had gotten away from you.

I will never forget, I bid on a job and went over to take the test, and man, I'm prepared, you know, but nervous. When I walked in, the superintendent – not the superintendent, but the general foreman of the department, a guy named Koufax, he said, "You want to work over here?" I said, "Yeah." He went on to tell me about "Man, you've grease holes, you're down in the cellar and basement and stuff," and my response to him was -- I was clean just like you are now, because the job I had in the sewing room at that particular time was mostly pencil and paperwork, and I used to get clean kakis on, clean shirt and whatnot, and it was a good job, but you didn't make no money, but it was a good job, but anyhow, he said, "You can't work like that over here." I said, "Well, have you got anybody else doing it now?" He said, "Yeah." I said, "Well, I'm just as good as anybody you've got in here."

So, he sat down and he put the test down in front of me, and when he pulled this piece of paper out, it was a piece of paper about I guess six by eight and it had six problems on it, three plus four. I will never forget that as long as I live. It had a subtraction problem where you had to find -- you had to change your whole number, and it had a very simple problem. It had a simple multiplication table problem on there, and then you had a division problem and you had two fractions. You had to add a fraction and you had to subtract a fraction problem, find the least common denominator. The fraction problem was so simple, I did it in my head. Most of the tests I did in my head, all but the subtraction problem, I had to exchange one whole number to a fraction, and I was scared because when I saw the test, I said "It's got to be something more than this," because first I thought they were trying to trick me, because we knew they had situations where tests had been tampered with throughout the company, but when the deal went down, I said, "This is it?" He said, "Yeah." He said, "You did good."

Then he went on, he said "Well, you know over here we work Saturdays, Sundays. They only had one day off a year that the mill don't run, and that's Christmas." I said, "Have you got anybody doing it now?" He said, "Yeah." I had known workers from before. We used to get off Labor Day, 4th of July. The sewing room was a pretty decent place to work. You just didn't make any money, and I went to work, and the guy -- I worked with guys who were white who couldn't read the morning's paper. I had one guy, he would help you over and above his duties because it was a team thing, operator, assistant operator, cooler and feeder. The assistant operator and feeder work together, and he would let the feeder write up the report, because you had to record all the information on the report from the cards, the coils, and it had to go up to the front. Somebody has wrote down a size or the weight and the coil number. That was the biggest thing about it. To make a long story short, he didn't have an education. He was an assistant operator, but they were saying to me I had to have a high school diploma or a high school equivalency. I went to work then. That's where I retired--from the tandem team--making a decent living. Fortunate for me, I never got laid off again.

One of the things that helped me, I became vice-president of the union right after I got there, and they had super seniority for lay-off purposes in the contract, so that kept me from getting laid off. It worked out pretty good.

I remember when I went in to the sewing room and started, you have a bathroom here and a bathroom here, black, white. We had a bunch of females in our area. They protected those females. No black females, all white females was working in the sewing room when I started. When I became vice-president, I will never forget, the assistant superintendent came to me, said, "Ed, we've got to do something." He said this black bathroom -- now, in one situation, it was just the matter of a wall, a wall here and a door on this side and a door on that side. You went into the bathroom or rest rooms is actually what they were. There was no difference in the facilities. It wasn't like they had air condition or better soap or anything. They had the same type materials and stuff, which leads me to another situation that we were in.

When I was working in the sewing room, it had like eight stools or commodes. We had toilets and you had commodes, and the white bathroom, they must have had 15, 16 commodes, and sometimes you would be working, you would have to go to the bathroom. You stop your job and you run to the bathroom. Well, periodically some of those commodes would be broke, stopped up or whatever, they weren't working, and you had to stand there. So, at that particular time, I went "I'm going in the white bathroom." So that went on -- I got a bunch of other guys to do the same thing. All of us was somewhat reluctant, but again, like I said, I thought I was -- I'm bad, thought I was bad anyhow. One of the guys, I will never forget it, they used to work with my father. At first, he thought I was a nice boy, and when he saw me in the white bathroom a couple of times, he said, "What happened, what are you doing in here?" I said, "What difference does it make? A bathroom is a bathroom." Like I said, I was smart and snotty, and he said, "What happens if somebody catches you and they jack you up and hang you up to the ceiling?" I said, "You ain't got enough people in here to do that to me."

I felt that good about myself, and he said well -- but what I did, I immediately went to the assistant superintendent of the tin mill, and I told him what had happened, and I told him why -- a part of the reason I'm a crane hooker, at that time I was a crane hooker. I've got to keep these tables loaded for these women. Periodically, I have to go to the bathroom, and sometimes the bathrooms, the commodes in the black bathroom are broke, and we have to stand and wait, and I said, "Well, I don't have time to wait, I've got to keep my tables loaded," and I told him what happened, that this guy had threatened to hang me up. He says, "I know it's hard." The assistant superintendent, a man named Bill Morgan, he says, "I know it's hard, but if they put their hands on you, you don't do nothing, you come to me and let me fight your battle for you." Now wait a minute, hold it. If somebody is trying to hurt me, I'm going to try to hurt them back. I guess I was like 23, 24 years old. And he says, "I'm telling you," but what they did, they fixed all the commodes the next day. He put a directive out and they fixed all the commodes, and they kept them fixed so that that conflict wouldn't develop, but that was like prior to '64 when they first filed discriminating charges.

Okay. The one they are showing down in there, my next-door neighbor, it's a couple of doors just hired, got hired down there and he was telling me that they showed a movie. He said, "Oh, that's my neighbor, Mr. Bartee," because we did several things with Jack Robinson to show where management and the union was working together trying to reduce the man hours per ton, that was the goal in those days.

They came out with all kinds of changes -- the first thing they came out with around 1971, '72 in the contract, was what was called a productivity committee. Bob and I eliminated jobs, which there was some positives there in the sense that they had crew size and things there that were obsolete. They had people doing things that I thought wasn't really necessary. It was – let me give you an example. I worked on the housing line, the Electroplate line. If something went wrong with the mill, the operator would make a decision--is that mechanical or electrical, and let's say for the sake of discussion he says, "It's electrical." The electrical guy would come and look at it, and he says, "No, it's mechanical." Then the mechanical guy would come. The electrical guy would go on back to the shop. Well, okay, let's say we're going to change our roll. Then you've got to call the electrical guy back to take the power off the line. Then you've got to send and get what they call motor inspectors to take the heads off the motors off the rolls. Then the mechanic takes the roll out, puts it back in. Then at that point, the motor specialist had to come back to put the head on. Then the electrical people come back and put the power on. Then you've got to send for oil or greaser to grease the burns because it's a new roll, you pump oil in it.

All this is a delay, when actually all it could be done by two or three people, and when they deal with that, you are using like four different job classes of people to get it done. Those were the type of things that the productivity, the green book, the LMP, Labor Management Participation, those were some of the things that management was attempting and trying to negotiate their way through it. If they filed a grievance -- there were some grievances filed in other companies where the company said "Okay, we don't need this guy anymore" and they kicked him out, but the work was there and they assigned the work to other people that was already there, and so grievances had been lost, and what management was trying to do was to negotiate their way through it, and of course, the union politics is one thing and reality is another thing.

Then out of that came management so that sometimes you had coordinators, and the coordinators were basically the people who worked in the mill who had never coordinated workloads. Now they have got a chance to work in the office, don't have to kill themselves, bundles of overtime and stuff like that and it was abused. Like I say, they tried three or four different ways to get it, and they are still doing it, trying to negotiate themselves out of jobs that were redundant, unnecessary jobs.

When my dad worked there and when I was a kid, I thought it was a great place to work for a couple of reasons. I remember during World War II my dad worked in there, and he was working seven days a week, 12 hours a day. Yeah, he walked right in from I and J Street to the mill. If he overslept or something like that, he would get up and go to work, my mother would fix his lunch, and I would take his lunch over to the police booth.

You know about Bethlehem Steel owned their own fire department, own police department. They were nice, they would call down the mill. I would give them my father's badge number. They would call down the mill, he would come up, I would give him his lunch. In some cases, I might leave it at the booth--depends on how much time I had. It was a good place to work.

Again, blacks didn't make a lot of money. I can remember my father coming home and raving about how many tons of steel he had run or pounds of steel, and he was feeding the machine making angles. I didn't know what the job was at that particular time, but once I went to work, I went to work in the same area where he worked at, and there was some of the people saying, "You are Ernest Bartee's son?" "Yes, I'm Ernest's son." This is the job he used to do.

Then I started asking some questions about -- it wasn't a piecework thing where they made tons. It was a thing where he was competing against his next-door neighbor, and I mean in the real sense. His next-door neighbor was a guy

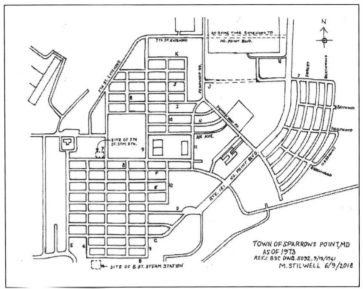

Map of the Town of Sparrows Point--courtesy Mike Stillwell

named Jack Winn. He lived at 803. We lived at 805, and Mr. Jack Winn would always try to outwork daddy. But that was their thing, but it wasn't -- they had a good foreman. My father didn't do too much of it, but there were guys who would go hunting, bring the general foreman a rabbit back, go fishing, bring fishes back. If your wife was a good cake maker or a pie maker or something like that, you would take the general foreman a pie and stuff like that. He looked out for them in those days. He would take some of the crew people -- some of the general foreman and some of the superintendents, not all of them, would send guys to their house to cut the grass, clean out the garage, do domestic jobs that had to be done. I can recall -- my daddy really never complained about the discrimination portion of it.

I can remember him arguing with neighbors about the union going in, in '41, '42, yeah. I don't remember the year, but I know the year now because of my background as far as the union at Sparrows Point, but I was a little boy, and I remember when the union -- the shipyard was trying to get a union in Sparrows Point shipyard, and my mother had a cousin, living with us, because in those days a lot of guys would come from the south, work with the intention of making enough money to buy a farm, go back home and live, and my wife had a cousin who did that, and he went across the line that they had, and I will never forget. He had a big old hunting knife. He says, "If they mess with me, I'm going to hook them with this here." I can remember that, I was a young boy, didn't really realize what was going on, but I can remember the struggle when they brought the union in.

My father was from Farmville, Virginia, and just moved up here looking for work and settled in Sparrows Point. I'm the oldest. My oldest brother, he worked there, and he had a stroke and had a heart attack and died early. My next brother worked there. My next brother, he didn't go to Sparrows Point. He made a career out of the service, and then my other brother, he worked construction work, he never worked in the steel mill at Sparrows Point. Then my baby brother worked for the railroad, and just retired a couple of years ago. None of my sisters ever worked at the steel mill. In those days, they didn't allow black women in the steel mill.

When I got out of high school, really my goal was to start a trucking business. I had a design to own trucks, to go into the trucking business. I had a cousin who went to college who was studying to be a doctor and I always said, "Man, by the time you get finished school I will have enough trucks on the road, I will make more money than you have," but unfortunately my wife got pregnant and instead having one kid, we kept on multiplying, and those were my trucks, that's what happened.

We had six trucks. My oldest son worked at the Point. Well, he drowned about 10, 15 -- '87 he died. Almost 20 years ago, 15, 16 years ago. He worked there, that's the only two sons I have. My daughter had a ball, she worked there during the summer. She went to college, and she worked there during a couple of summers, but none of the rest of the kids. My baby boy, when they were hiring back a couple of years ago, I said, "Do you want to get a job at the Point?" I was in a position to help him. "I don't want to work there, dad." I think they didn't like the idea of working Saturdays and Sundays and shift work.

It's interesting to talk to people about families and questions of whether people would do it again. You were together on third shift, you were snowed in down there, and in addition to working together, there were a lot of what the guys called steelworker widows, that put Christmas dinner on by themselves because the husband was working down at the mill.

I guess lucky for me, like I said, by me being in the tin mill, I never missed a Christmas from being with my family. I think I had worked one New Year's Eve the whole time I was down there when I was in the mill when the new year came in. Because of the tin mill, they shut down because eventually-- I had mentioned earlier that you couldn't, the only day they shut the mill down was Christmas. Then as time went on, orders came from the north, they start shutting the mills down more often, and so that made it a little bit better. Of course, I went to work at the union hall. They gave me a little latitude to sort of make my own schedule to a degree, and it made it much easier for me.

My uncle, Vernon Bartee, was the zone committeeman before I went into the mill, in the tin mill, sewing room. In the tin mill, he was the zone committeeman. He would say "Come on to the union meeting." Okay, he had helped me got the job. He was the reason I got the job, where I was. In those days, you go to the general foreman "I've got a son, cousin, et cetera," and give him your name, they call you and tell you to go to the employment office, you've got the job.

So, he said "Come to the union meeting." I will never forget, I went to the union meeting, and at the time I went to the union meeting, the Democratic Convention was going on TV, and they were raising hell, screaming "Mr. Chairman" and all that sort of stuff. Well, the union meeting room reminded me of that. When I went to the union meeting, they were hollering and screaming and calling each other liars and all that kind of stuff, you know. Well, hey, I like action, you know, and I started going to union meetings.

This was local 2609, up on Dundalk Avenue, and this was '55, '56. Like I said, I started going to union meetings. I got active, and I joined a group called the "Statesmen." That was a group that was attempting to eliminate discrimination. I started going to union meetings -- my uncle was well liked, he was one of the boys.

A guy named Chris Loucas was president of the local then. At that particular time when I first started, Chris Loucas' ticket was for real, and, as a result, I liked him, and I started listening and learning and I started going to shop steward classes. I had never been a shop steward, elected shop steward, put it that way. I would go and I would tell the guys, "Hey, man, they are messing over you," and I would tell them why and make them put pressure on the shops to get things done.

We had an election, and I ran for delegate to the convention, and I took my car and I was hauling people from Sparrows Point and Turner Station to the union hall and rode all day long. At this time, I was living in Sparrows Point. All day long, because I knew in order to work at the Point you had to live there and in order to live on the Point, you had to work at the Point. And I knew a lot of people at Turner Station and Sparrows Point, I was raised up there, and I was like "Man, I need your vote." Well, my ticket lost because they had the green ticket and the blue ticket. My ticket lost, but I was the highest vote getter on my ticket, and when they got ready for election of officers, one group came to me and said, "Hey man, they want to make you vice-president." You are crazy, because I really hadn't had any union experience other than just going to the union hall.

I had done some appointments, I worked as a teller, worked as a secretary of the education committee. They had a couple of Christmas parties, things like that, I worked on those things, but I really hadn't had any deep exposure to negotiating and grievance solving. I mean, you've got to be kidding. He said "No, everybody spoke very highly of you," and in those days I kept myself clean, always did, looked well when I went out and dressed as far as I was concerned, and they gave me compliments.

At that particular time, the union had decided that we wanted to have two blacks in the top five, that's what really brought it on. They brought a group that was in the office and said "Look, we need to do something," and they had a black treasurer and they wanted me for vice-president as a black. Well, we got together with the other group, and there was a blue ticket and a green ticket, and we told them what happened, and a couple of times, they had ran on the green ticket they had a black vice-president, white president. On the blue ticket, they had -- they didn't have any blacks or they might have had just one black in the treasurer's position, and the guy from the green ticket would win with the blue ticket. In other words, you have a Democratic president with a Republican vice-president, because they would split the ticket.

So, we got together. I got with Lee Douglas. He was a part of the other group. I said "They are offering me vice-president," and I said "You know what they did to a guy named John Haus, they cut John Haus, but I said if you've got a black vice-president on your ticket and we've got a black vice-president on our ticket, that makes it even playing ground. We've got two blacks in the top five." And so, it worked, I beat Haus. Lee Douglas ran. Douglas was a much smarter man than I am or I was. He knew more about the contract, he had a couple years of college education, but he was advocate of civil justice. He would take the union floor and talk about how they were discriminating when it was very, very unpopular. So as a result, once I got in, I applied myself, and they ran -- I ran against white guys. Every election that we had I won two to one, three to one. Even a couple situations we stole the guy away from the thing with the black and white, black and white. They kept trying to maintain that. Once or twice, couple of times there they didn't have a black in the position, I still walked away with it.

The thing that helped me the most was during the 70's and the 80's, unemployment was extremely high and the system with the state wasn't a good system. People were six, seven, eight, ten checks behind, weren't getting the checks on time, and they gave me an assignment to work with unemployment, help get the checks. I became a household word, and it lasted for -- oh, my goodness. I will tell you what, I was in office for 32 years, never lost an election, either president or vice-president. I lost within the party. I ran for president, I lost that, but then they picked me up for vice-president, but as far as the general election is concerned, I never lost one.

But the thing that helped me a whole lot -- I meet people today, and you talk to a couple of guys, guys that I don't know, say "Man, I remember you, you helped me." I don't remember who they were, because in those days I would have 75, 100 tracers going downtown just about every day, finding out "Why hasn't this guy gotten his check, what can we do to help him," and what we did, we took care of that, bring cards back, call him up or I stop by his house and say "Look, fill out this card out, turn them in tomorrow, and you'll have a check within three or four days." I did a lot of that.

Then I got to the point where, if he was denied benefits, I was what they called the Philadelphia Lawyer. I conducted hearings before the hearing officer, and then from there I went to the Board of Review. I conducted hearings on both levels. I won quite a few cases, because, at that particular time, I knew more about the contract than the company guy that they had. Some of the stuff that they were trying to do was just wrong and I knew it was wrong. We would show the state where it was wrong, and it worked for me. Then I conducted some Social Security disability hearings, I won a few of them, too. I lost a few, but I won a few, too. So as a result, that helped me develop a name for myself throughout the union.

Now I don't remember the 1946 strike my Dad went through, but 1959-- that was the last big strike. The '59 strike, I was chairman of the education committee, chairman or secretary, I forgot now, but what they did, all your committees like the standing committees, all those people were given responsibilities to do certain things, so I worked in the store. Other guys worked in the kitchen, you know, fixing food, but I worked in the store. At that store, they gave out food to help the people. Other guys worked on the rent thing, other guys that worked on utilities, gas, electric bills and stuff like that, but mine was the store. It was a fun thing. We were able to save a few hundred dollars. I think it was 14 or $1,500 when we went out on strike, which was a lot of money in those days. The food they gave us when I was working in the store, we got a little extra because nobody got paid. The strike -- it was fun, because you worked every other day. Some weeks I had to work every day, because I had to load and unload the trucks, but we had a lot of fun. The fun came in when you was unloading the trucks and fixing boxes and stuff, we were selling cardboard and buying beer. A couple of the guys, one of the guys had a truck, that was their assignment. You take all the cardboard boxes, and they come back with 10, 12 cases of beer, and then some of the places like Mickey's, I know you've heard of Mickey's, and Amoco, and various bars where steelworkers hung out, they were donating beer for the steelworkers.

Because they got kind of shaky there, I think must have been around -- gee, oh, boy, tenth week, somewhere in that ballpark, maybe a little bit later. This guy came down -- one of the zone committeeman, a guy named Jack O'Ryan, he lived in Highlandtown, and he knew this loan company, financing. I will never forget it because I never made a loan. I didn't know anything about interest at that particular time, and he said, "Just go up there and tell them I sent him." So, my wife and I said "Well, let's go get this loan." So, we went to get a $300 loan, and all we did was put it in the bank because at that particular time, we were still living off the $1,400. I will never forget this as long as I live, the first payment, my payment was $21. They put $14 in interest and $7 on the principle. Man, I had a fit, but my hands were tied because the first payment, I was still on strike, and right after that, they settled, we went back to work. We had the cooling period, and we went back to work. And as we got back to work and when everything was settled, I filed my taxes and I just went on and paid the loan off. I kept the $300 in the bank, but it was interesting to be out there without a job. I had three kids at that particular time, and I will never forget it, I had a car, making a car payment, and I went to the people at Commercial Credit, and they said well -- they looked at my record and they said well, because your record -- my payments were going, all I had to do was pay the interest for a few months, and the interest was $14, because I had gotten the payments down, they were that low.

And we had a lot of fun playing checkers, playing pinochle in the neighborhood. Again, we all still were living in Sparrows Point. They had about three places where it was a checker game, pinochle game, or go to the pool room, but there was always card games around, so it worked out good, and some of the people were less fortunate. I remember we used to have a guy come by who worked for the contractors, and the contractors weren't working during the strike, and I would give him a couple cans of food to help him out, but that's what the neighborhood was all about. If you were hungry down at Sparrows Point, your neighbors fed you, there was no problem.

In the strike, in those particular days, they were fighting for -- the company didn't want to give a decent raise, number one. Number two, insurance was the big thing. That was a big accomplishment out of that. They were able to get the company to pay for their insurance, healthcare benefit, because they used to have -- I will never forget it, the first pay they would take out the union dues. The third pay they would take out your insurance, your healthcare insurance. It wasn't a whole lot of money, but as time went on, it grew to be a big thing.

There was a lot of unanimity. I think people in those days appreciated the accomplishments of the union more so than they do now. You know, you walk in the mill now, you've got a holiday pay, you've got vacations, you've got your insurance paid for. One time we were getting 13 weeks vacation if you were a senior employee, every five years, one cycle, five-year cycle. The insurance and stuff that they have now, the improvements in the insurance benefits. We had at one point, the insurance -- and it still is among the top in the industry, in any industry, that the healthcare insurance that we have. It might have some problems, but it's still a good plan.

To teach the younger generation of workers about the union, we have to do just what we are doing now, talk, talk, talk about the conditions, the way they were and the way they are now. When I started working there for example --and I want to get it right. I think the shift premium was three percent on 3:00 to 11:00 and seven percent on 11:00 to 7:00, and I think it's up to what; ten and fifteen now. I'm not sure, I forgot.

It was increased. I think once you just sit and talk to people about how the struggle was and what you went through. Let them know that one of the other things is, I think, we do a lot of teaching the people how not to work and let me explain what I mean by that. There are a lot of jobs where you've got an assignment, you've got to get so much accomplished, and when people come in the mill a lot of times they take and teach those people how to do the job, get it done right away, and you are free the rest of the day. As a result when new employees come in, they get exposed to not working instead of working. I think that doesn't help them much. I'm not saying you've got to work your ass off for eight hours a day, but I think I always believe a fair day's work for a fair day's pay, and they need to talk about the conditions.

There were certain situations that were unsafe. For example, like when I first started in the electrical department, we had little box cars with soda ash, and we had to load those with hand. You pile them up on the skid, and they would take them with a tractor from the box car, carry them to the soda ash room, and we would stack them up, and that stuff would get on you, you would sneeze all day long. You worked a lot harder than they work today, a whole lot harder. Towards the end, soda ash started coming out on skids, so all you do was stack the skids on top of each other. We used to have what's called pigs, it's actually pure tin. Those things weighed anywhere from 80 to 90 pounds. We had pick them up, put them on the skid, take them to the room and then stack them again. Now they come in on box cars, always banded up and everything, and it's just a matter of the tractor going and picking it up.

There were a lot of jobs like that where it was hard work, a lot of sweeping and stuff. You had long areas to sweep, but they had a lot of sweepers in to take the place of that, so there was a lot of stuff, like the banding of coils. Used to be a time where everything was manual. Now they've got machines that do two-thirds of that stuff. You worked a lot harder in the old days, and the only thing you can do is tell the young people is how over a period of time, some of the improvements came as a result of the employees making recommendations to management, and some of the management brought in new ideas themselves, you know.

I remember when we would work eight hours and probably bend three or four coils, because in those days most of the stuff was going out there cut, but we banded up three or four coils, and then you had a hoist with a chain on it, you had to pull it. You couldn't do no better, but as a result now they do what, 700 to 800 coils a day band, but those are the things that a lot of the people in the mill have forgotten about, because let's face it, you are talking 30 years ago, 35 years ago those conditions at work existed.

For the future, I think they have got to do something about the legacy card. If they get some help from the Government to do with a legacy card, probably develop a new type of pension program, maybe a 401K and do something with the redundant jobs and do something with the foreign imports. Now, they have got a tariff of 30 percent for the next three or four years. If they can get that -- get some type of limit on imports, foreign exports, they can turn it around, they can do good. I think what's going on over there now, if Bethlehem Steel would have diversified in a more positive manner -- they tried some things, but they never really, really got the thing off the ground like they were supposed to. They had a supply of ten --they had warehouses in a couple places in the country, they didn't stick with that. U.S. Steel is financially solvent, they diversified. What they did different from Bethlehem, I don't know. They had a lot more things going for them than Bethlehem did. And to be honest with you, when Bethlehem made money, everybody got some goodies, so I think that was one of the things.

I keep active by being on the Board of Directors for the credit union. Most of the guys still work, like Chuck Swearingen, for example, and Jerry Ernest. I can't think -- I've got a couple other guys' names. But anyhow, we talk about it, and then when we go to -- find a secretary for the retirees club in 2609 and we have the officers come in periodically and give us a report as to what's going on in the mill, and then when I bump into Eddie, my son, I ask him questions, and just more or less hearsay, whatever you pick up in the paper and that's where I get most of my information from.

Oh, yeah, I guess just about every day I hear from guys who are retired. I get a phone call maybe two or three times a week, "Hey, man, what's going on, what's going to happen with our insurance, what's going to happen with our pension," and I try to stay on top of it to help the guys, because when I first came off, I was still doing problem solving, people calling me. A lady called me the other day, wanted to rent the union hall. "Well, you helped me ten years ago." "Well, sweetheart, I'm not there anymore, call Ed, Jr." "Oh, your son, okay," and that works out. But like I said, my wife was telling me yesterday when I went to an anniversary party during the day, one of the steelworkers, a guy was 92 years old. She said a guy called and wanted to know about insurance. She said, "He's going to call me back." Well, he hasn't called back. So those things I know I will tell you. Those I don't know, I don't give out bad information.

Eddie Bartee, Sr. and Eddie, Jr—2018—Turner Station

I'm proud of my son working at The Point. I fought with him to go to college, he didn't want to go to college. Keep in mind 30 years ago a guy could go in the steel mill and make more than a professor at the university at Morgan [State University]. I had a brother-in-law that attended Morgan. I was making more money as a feeder on the tandem line than he was as a professor. Made more money than a school teacher. I can recall going to a PTA meeting. My wife used to always go to PTA meetings, and this teacher came to me -- at that particular time, I was fresh in the union, and she knew about it and she said "my brother-in-law said he made so much money by working Thanksgiving Day," and I said "yeah, he was right," and I remember in those days you could make -- if you worked double time on a holiday, you could make yourself $250, $300, somewhere in that ballpark, and that's what he had made. She couldn't understand that, because she was working as a school teacher, probably making $50 a day, and this is back in the 70's or 80's, late 70's, early 80's. She said, "Why?" She thought he was lying, because he came home, they had Thanksgiving dinner at his house, and he was saying how much money he had made that day. I said, "Yeah." She said, "Oh my goodness, I'm in the wrong business, I shouldn't be teaching. Maybe I should work in the steel mill." So that was a challenge. Eddie had a couple buddies who had gone to work at the steel mills before him, and they were talking "Man, look at the money you can make."

Things were much better for him than they were for me. I guess when Eddie started working in the steel mill, laborers were probably making $6, $7 an hour, which was pretty good money, so he was happy. He did pretty good for himself. I never had a problem with him not going to work, missing a whole lot of time or going to work being two-cent sick or something like that. He's a typical young man who did everything he could to get out of work, I won't argue that with you, but needless to say, now he's chosen it, and he caught on, he is doing much better than I thought he would have done as early as he did, let's put it that way. I'm proud of him.

I did pretty much the civil rights movement in the plant. When they were doing the thing about integration in restaurants and stuff like that, I did a few demonstrations, but I was hot-headed, and they were preaching nonviolence. They had a couple situations where people would spit on people going into the five and dime downtown where they were trying to integrate, and I made the statement, "Man, if that would have been me, I would have knocked his head off." I didn't go. That was part of the reason I didn't go, because I was sort of what you call -- but as far as the steel, I worked real hard on the steel mill thing, because what happened, I was a black officer in the local union when they first started that, and when Pittsburgh sent their people in to see what was going on, they were directed to black leaders, and we had several meetings and stuff and explained the conditions to them as to what was going on.

I met Francis Brown during that time. I didn't know him before we started the struggle. This guy Lee Douglas, you've got to meet Lee Douglas. Lee was -- they had a group of four friends, the Brown group, called the Statesman. That was the group that I belonged to at first, and then we went from the Statesman to Steelworkers for Equality. Then Francis and them, they went out and they got CORE, Congress for Racial Equality, something like that, and those boys, so they started -- our group was dealing with the NAACP. Francis' group was dealing with CORE, and as a result they wound up putting their efforts together, and we were able to get some gainful -- some positive.

We took up a collection and agreed that they would send two people from 2609 and two people from 2610 to take some money to Johnstown, the flood area to give some relief. When we got there, the guys were over at this like a Moose Hall, and one of the guys carried us over there, and when we went in there, there was a long hallway. Like we came to the door there, and down the hall was the entrance to the bar and the restaurant portion of it, and when we got there, you had to ring the bell to get there. So, when we got there, the guy opened the door and said, "Hold it, stay right here." I will never forget that. In the meanwhile, they went in there and they got the guys that we wanted to see. He said, "Okay, come on. Let's go." The guys said, "Where are we going?" He said, "We will get you something to eat."

There was two blacks and two whites from Baltimore that had gone up to deliver the check, myself being one of them, and we learned this later on that no black man had ever been beyond them doors. There was discrimination, and I felt bad about it in a way and I felt good. I said well -- because they wanted to carry us on a tour to see how the water had washed trailers all up on the banks and stuff, it really put a hurt on them. That was an interesting experience.

Would I do it again? Yeah, I wouldn't have no problem. I've been blessed. All my kids completed high school. Those that wanted to go to college --three of them went to college. I own my home, got a couple dollars in the bank. My wife and I do traveling. I completed high school and compared on average to the average guy in my category, guys I worked with, I'm comfortable. I feel blessed.

Tony Buba, Eddie Bartee, Len Shindel--2018

I feel good about it, and I guess the interesting part about that I never realized how much I was appreciated until after I retired, and I started roaming around and people were speaking at the Montebello Lake. *Beaucoup* of steelworkers that go around the Lake Montebello "How are you, Bartee," and I would speak and get an opportunity to talk to them, like "Well, where do you know me from." I will be looking down. "Well, you did this for me." I had people in 2610 who would come over to me and get me to help them with their unemployment problems. I feel I was able to help some people, and one of the greatest thrills I've had -- I mentioned to you earlier I came from a small neighborhood.

My father got sick a lot, he had pneumonia, he had an eye operation and stuff like that, and whenever he got sick, people would take offerings, I mean collections -- offerings are in church--take up collections or either they would buy us a ton of coal or a guy would deliver a ton of coal and stuff like that, we got a lot of help. Up until about three or four years ago, every time somebody asked for something, I would give it to them because I would see people on the street, I give them a dollar, 50 cents, whatever change I had, because I was blessed that people helped us.

As a result, one of the best things I did-- I went to work one Monday morning and they said "Ed, help him. Do what you can to help him," and the guy had come down here from Philadelphia on a weekend spree with a couple of buddies of his--his buddy had relatives living here and they said they were hiring at Sparrows Point, and he went down to Sparrows Point. They didn't go back to Philadelphia. He went down to Sparrows and he got a job. He didn't know a living soul in Baltimore. He was able to bunk with some of his buddies' people for a little while. Then he had to bring his wife and kids here, and that was in the early stage. He got sick and didn't have any money, and he couldn't get a check from Bethlehem Steel, because he had a form that had to be filled out, and he didn't have enough money to pay the doctor to fill the form out. It was called a pink slip, and I said okay, we went to the doctor, University Hospital. We got the doctor to fill the form out. I called the company. The company said, "Ed, if you bring the form here, we will write him a check."

There used to be laundry workers who had a place up on Rowan Avenue. So, for some reason I stopped by there. I don't know why I stopped by there, but anyhow I was telling what I was doing. The lady, her name was Betty Brown, she said, "Well, we can help him." She got him two big bags of groceries. I gave him money to buy cigarettes with, and I gave him money to put in his pocket, like five dollars, something, it wasn't a whole lot of money. Cigarettes were much cheaper in those days. Got him a couple packs of cigarette, put some money in his pocket, change for him to go to work. His check was ready the next day. That was Tuesday, I picked his check up and I carried it to him, and that was the best feeling that I had as far as really, really helping, and he had money to get his medicine, he got his pink slip and got things going on.

The guy came to me, I guess, about two years later, and I forgot all about it. I didn't forget the situation, but I had forgotten who he was, what he looked like. He told me who he was. He wanted to buy me a sandwich. I said, "No, man." He said, "I've got to give you something." What he did -- I was smoking then. He came by, I was smoking Viceroy cigarettes. He came back with five packs of Viceroy and threw them on my desk. "You helped me, you take them," you know.

And I had a couple other situations. I will never forget I was at Mickey's one day, I was running late, and I very seldom eat at Mickey's, very seldom I eat fast food. On this particular day I stopped at Mickey's and ate a sandwich, and I got ready -- sandwich, bowl of soup. I ate the soup, I ate the sandwich, I'm going down the road to get to a meeting. This guy ran up to me. I had my hand in my pocket. "Don't take his money," and he threw a ten-dollar bill up. I said "Man." He said, "Man, you got my check for me. I had called that place and called that place. They kept giving me the run around. I called you and in less than three days' time my check was there." He said, "I want to do something for you."

I had those kinds of experiences. I retired in ninety-six. I was there forty-one years, plus.

Mary Lorenzo
February, 2006

I grew up in Cockeysville, and I was married and had three children. I divorced, and I went to work at Westinghouse in Cockeysville and meanwhile, then, I remarried, and I got pregnant and I thought "I have worked all my life, I'm going to stay home." Well, I just couldn't be a Suzie homemaker, I just don't like that, you can tell, but I just didn't like that.

I liked physical work, and a friend of mine had moved in these old apartments in Essex across from Salvo's--they are torn down now--and one of my neighbors, her husband worked at the shipyard, and she said "My husband said they are hiring at Bethlehem Steel, the steel mill, do you want to go down there," and I said "Yes." So we went down, it was in 1971, April of 1971, and I made less money at Bethlehem Steel on turn work than I made at Westinghouse when I left there, but that's how I got started, and I would get laid off and stuff, but it didn't bother me at that time because I was married.

And then when my second husband and I broke up, you know, I couldn't take these layoffs, so I transferred over to the steel side, and it was me and a lady, Mary Denny, she is deceased now. She had to go back to work because she was single, to get the benefits for her children, and we went to the employment office, and they said the only place we have for you is the batteries, and we are thinking "car batteries." Well, what can be bad with batteries? They are saying, "Oh, they are terrible," and I can remember Mary and I, we signed up, we went to work. So, we go to the steel side -- now, we had been on the finishing side all this time and you know how the parking lots are.

Well, when we got to the steel side, we parked and we start walking, we had to go to the coke ovens, and we are walking and walking and we are saying to everybody "How do you get to the coke ovens," they said, "Keep going down here." We are walking, we said "They are giving us the runaround, they don't want women here." We didn't realize how far you had to walk. I mean you had to walk, and I guess it was around '73 --no, I think '76. Anyway, around '78 or something before they had a bus that would pick you up and take you, but I mean it was a long walk.

And I went into the labor gang, I went on to the batteries, and it was the hardest work--they put me in the mud mill. The batteries were where they made the coke, and it was like, I guess, coal comes -- I don't know how they do it, but they had a machine on top that would go over and would drop this coal, I guess, down into the holes, and that would bake for so long, and then they had like one machine on one side that would be a pusher and it would line up to the door, and at that time they had mud – they had men that did the mudding, and then on the other side would be the catcher, and it would push that ramrod right on through.

But I worked in the mud mill, and you would go out and you would clean these runs. When they would push that coke out, you would have to go with a wheelbarrow and a shovel and all and load it in the wheelbarrow and take it back. There was a big round thing, a prehistoric big round thing that had a wheel that went like this and water, and you threw this coke in there and you went down below, and you got clay, you put clay in there, and it would mix it into a mud. As it came into the mud, then I think you opened it up like a little trough, and it would shoot out on the floor, and on seven and eight batteries -- they had up to twelve. I worked five and six I think it was, but anyway, seven and eight, people on five and six or three and four would have to make the mud for seven and eight. I don't know why they didn't have a mud mill, but when I first went there the guy said "Here's your job."

Well, I stuck my shovel in that mud, Bill, and I couldn't pull it out, the suction was holding it, and at the end of the day I would have a pile about that big on that shovel, because it killed you, but you made mud. You had to make so many batches of mud, and then I think around two o'clock, that was the last time you had to have your mud made, and that was the last until the next shift--it was clear for like two hours. So, with the guys, I was slowing them down. I mean, I was working, but I was slowing them down, so we made a deal--I would go out and clean all the runs because they made their last batch of mud, I think, like at one o'clock, and I would go clean the runs so they were finished at 1:00, and they knew that I would do all that.

And so finally I went to Johnny Fair, I went in to get off because, like I said, my son at that time, my oldest son, was in Stembridge Football League, and I wanted to go see the games, and on the batteries, you worked turn work. I can remember going to Johnny Fair and going up to -- I can't remember who the superintendent was at the coke ovens--and he said "Boy, you just -- you have too much of an outside life. Maybe you just better quit, you've got too much going on outside."

So, there were guys that wanted to get on the batteries because they made the money. The yard gang just cleaned up the coke that fell on the ground and stuff like that. So that's what happened. I had more seniority

Johnny Fair

than a lot of them so that's how, when I wanted to get off, I got out. That's what saved me with Johnny. I have to say, Johnny did fight for me, maybe toward the end, you know, after everybody start seeing it, the picture changed, and everything was fine, I didn't complain about anything. I mean other than, you know, the flirting and the stuff like that, but, I mean, I could handle that.

It was just when I went into the crafts, and I mean it wasn't just me, Paula Bouche was in there before me in refrigeration, and I mean it was awful, awful, and the guys -- there were some guys that were really good friends of mine and they seen what was being done to me, but it was just like that movie [*North Country*]. The only person who stuck up for me was Dave Fenwick, and the foreman had the police come over and took his locker out and swore that his locker hadn't been in there, you know, retaliated against him and all, and Dave transferred out -- this was in the late '90s I guess or 2000. Dave transferred out and went into -- I don't know if it was the bull gang or the pipe fitters or something. I'm saying '79 was when I went into the crafts. There was positions opened for electrical helpers over at ERS and refrigeration, and I had gone over and taken the electrical helper's test and all and passed it. When I went over to the employment office, it was a gentleman at that time named Mr. Holland, and he was really nice, and I was telling him, you know, why I wanted this job, and he says, "Well, Mary, the best job is the refrigeration." He said, "But the only trouble is you've got the worst boss in the world." He said that was Larry Reece, and I thought "Well, I can go over there," and when I went over there, I didn't really -- Larry was one of these ones that really hollered at you, but he never held a grudge or anything, you know. You just had to take him. He was nice, I liked him, and you knew where you stood with him.

But it was some of the men, one of the guys -- when I see that with her with her cigarette, when he reached in her pocket [in the movie *North Country*], that's what this one guy would do to me all the time. One time him and I went down on one of the blast furnaces that was shut down. I didn't know, you know, I just went in there. I knew that, in the winter, we did maintenance on different things, but I didn't know, and we went on this blast furnace and it was shut down, and he bends down, Bill, and his whole privates, everything is hanging out. It's the God's truth, and all we were doing was changing the filter. I mean I didn't even see him. Put the things on, he got up and went on out to the truck. I would tell my friend, who was Bob Arrowood, his wife worked there in the machine shop, and she cried all the time, you know, the way they did to her over there, but I could handle that.

Then when they got the boss, and I wouldn't want to mention his name, but when we got this one particular boss, he made me -- it was a living hell for me. I mean absolutely -- he would make me wash the trucks, and it wasn't like I didn't mind washing the trucks, but he would stand out there and watch me, and it was just awful with him.

And when I went into the last job I had, I had a general foreman named Norman Miller, and right before I retired, right before I went out sick, Norman Miller told me that when I first came over -- I could tell when I came there how the foremen were watching me, you know, and stuff, and he told me that this foreman told him that I wasn't any good, I wouldn't work, I was nothing but to stir up trouble, and everything. He told me, he says, "You know, Mary, I have never found you to be that way," but that's what this foreman, you know, and I don't know what else. I would have to speak good of everything I did down there except in the crafts, and it's just like that movie, and I mean the girls up in the locker rooms, they knew it.

We talked about it in the locker rooms. Oh, yeah, everybody knew, everybody knew the shit they put me through in refrigeration. Oh, you want to hear about the telephone call. That was in I think '82. I got sent to Pennwood Power, and, like I said, I went in the electrical department, I was scared to death of electricity. Well, I couldn't get any worse than down there in the powerhouse, but I was working in the powerhouse. This one guy from ERS, the lineman, they had sent him too, and he told them he couldn't climb, and he was going to bump me because he had more seniority. I remember the general foreman called me upstairs, and he was on the phone and he says, "What is he going to do, what is he going to come over here and tell us he can't do the job?" and he had told me, he said, "Mary, you know, do everything you can."

So, when I went out there, Steve Stahoviak -- have you ever heard him? He said, "Girl, get them hooks on because you are going to climb a pole." I said, "Oh, okay, I can climb a pole," and he says, "Real high." I said, "Well, I'm not afraid of heights. I climb on the cranes, you know." He says, "Well, this is nothing like a crane." Well, I always climbed trees. You know, I grew up in the country before I moved to Cockeysville. That's why I like that kind of work, and I climbed the pole. They brought me out and had all the men come, and I mean you are standing there, and it's not hard, it's all -- because you've got to be bowlegged, have your legs bowlegged get those spikes in. So, they had me do that on the first day, at the end of the day. I would say it was about 2:00.

So, the next day they sent me on a job, and they sent me with my foreman. I had a foreman, Mr. Cook, and they sent me over to, I think it was, third strand or one of those strands over there now, I can't remember, but he came down and he told me I had to go with him, I had to go climb, so I didn't know. It was him and another foreman and me, and they took me down, way down to the coke oven. I was all by myself, us three, and I didn't know to say "Hey, where is the union rep" or "Where is somebody else." I would go down there with them, and after I got involved, I knew it was their word against mine, that's why they did that.

So they told me to put the spikes on and climb up the pole and keep climbing until they told me to stop, and I couldn't have my belt, my belt was hanging down, but you know how they have them hooked when they are not around the pole. So I kept climbing, and I was getting up really high, and I knew you didn't have to touch that high voltage, just get so close, but I kept climbing. I guess they were waiting for me to say, "I'm scared" or something, but they said "Okay, you can come down."

Well, coming down, see, that's where I didn't shove that spike in far enough, and when I pulled the other one out, I cut out. Well, going up the pole you use the spikes, but they did have those hand things to hold on. So when I started to fall, my arms were going boom, boom, boom, and I grabbed ahold, but the rawhide on the spikes got caught around one of these hooks and my foot is up in the air like this and I am hanging like this and I couldn't get my foot undone, and I'm looking and I'm really psyching myself up, thinking now I'm going to fall, how can I push myself so I fall on my whole body instead of my head or my leg or something? And finally, I said to Mr. Cook, I said, "Cookie, I can't get my foot undone." After it all happened, I wouldn't have fallen because I would have dangled by my one leg there. He says, "Wait a minute," he came up and he said, "Can you give me your belt, "and like here I am, hanging, my foot up in the air. So, I lean my chest up against there, and I had my arm around and I unhooked it and then I grabbed – I brought it around. Of course, I had to hold on to here real quick, and he wouldn't hook it for me, I had to hook it myself, and then when I sat on my behind on my belt I got my hook undone, and I went on down the pole.

So, he says to me, "Do you want to go to the dispensary," and I said, "No." I said, "I know I bruised the hell out of myself," but I said, "I know nothing is broke," because it was just burning, and he said, "Okay."

So, they took me back to this job. I don't know what the position was, but what we were doing --they were running new cable, and that stuff is about that thick [2 inches], and they had put me on the job where they had the truck and they reeled it. Now I had to pull this cable and keep throwing it, but I had to make sure that I stayed away from him because this reel was going around, but it wasn't like you just hold it here, you had to keep it going, and I thought my chest was going to bust. I mean it was really -- where is the end of this cable? So, I did that, and at the end of the day, we go over to electrical construction, and, of course, the men all had bathrooms, and, of course, I didn't, but I didn't want to make a big stink, I just wore my clothes home. So, I forget--what was his name, Richard something? --he came, and he says to me, "You are laid off." This was on a Tuesday. I said, "I'm laid off? Why am I laid off?" He said, "You can't do the job," and I said to my foreman, I said, "Cookie, what did you ask me to do that I couldn't do?" And he said, "Mary, it's not me, it's higher up." So, I just started crying because I couldn't afford it with the kids. I'm hysterical crying, and to this day I don't know who it was, somebody came and said get to the dispensary.

So, I went flying over to dispensary, and I am just sobbing like a nut, and I see Bill Nugent, and I think it might have been -- I don't know if it was Eddie Bartee or there was another black gentleman I think that was in the union at that time. I know Bill Nugent.

But anyway, I stopped my car in the middle of the road when I see them, and I'm flagging them down, I mean, I am crying my eyeballs out. Bill goes, "What's wrong," and I told him that they laid me off. He said, "Well, they can't lay you off because you hurt yourself." I said, "They didn't lay me off because I hurt myself. They said they laid me off because I couldn't do the job."

So, I go in the dispensary. Well, they put me on SIP, so that saved me until a couple of days, I don't know. I would have been laid off Friday. They had another layoff, they knew it, it was just they were going to show me they were going to lay me off. So, Bill Nugent told me to go to Bernie Parrish, the chairman of the civil rights. He was the staff of civil rights. They said, "You know, she's a nut," but I went down to the EEOC, and they said to me "You need to go to the NLRB, I don't think your union is helping you," and I said, "Oh, I couldn't go against the union."

Well see, that's where, and I noticed this when I was the chairman of the civil rights, some of the things with the girls, they went into expediting positions. Now I know that the expediter in our shop was a male, and he had unlimited overtime. Now when these girls had it, it happened to be a white girl, and I went to Everett Hawkins, he was for [Local] 9116 then, and I said "Everett, they are discriminating against her, all the men." He says, "Don't start that word, I don't want to hear that word," and this is what made me angry because I remember a black girl calling up about changing her schedule or vacation or something, and the foreman says, "Oh, I don't have time to talk about this shit."

Well, they wanted to file this big suit, and it made me mad because you don't want to be divided, but they couldn't see what they were doing, you know. I mean, we were in the same place they were, and when I got in the mill, most of the times the black men were the nicest because they knew what you were going through, but the union, when you got to the union, you didn't find that. And people knew about it, but I went downtown because I didn't know all the procedures and everything, and I went downtown to the EEOC, but I also wrote letters to Lynn Williams [President of The Steelworkers International].

I wrote letters, I think, to Mr. Parrish. I think I just threw them away, I will look and see if I can find them there, but I wrote to him, and I went up to Dave Wilson, our District Director at the time, and I told Dave.

I belonged to 2610 at that time, and it was Walter Scott, and I'm trying to think who was -- GI Johnson was our civil rights man. He knew about it. I mean people knew about it because it was talked about, and I can't remember all the procedures, but after I got involved in the union, I realized what I done wrong. I didn't go and -- I didn't make that shop steward file a grievance and stuff. I went downtown, and at that time -- it wasn't on Center Place, it was somewhere else, right off of Franklin I think it was, and I went down there and I talked to an investigator, I think it was a Mr. Blue-- I talked to an intake worker and it was turned over to a Mr. Blue. And so they came and they investigated, and Bethlehem Steel said that everybody coming in that department that they started at a certain date they named a certain date--that everyone coming in there was required to climb, because a lineman is an apprenticeship program, you don't just go in there and become a lineman. So, I thought "Well, okay, if they didn't ask me to do anything more than anybody else."

I was talking to Bob Arrowood, and he was in my department then. Of course, I was laid off, they were working, and he said, "Me and Melvin were over there after that and we were there for six months." He said, "We never climbed." He said, "In fact, they kept saying to Melvin 'Hey, if you don't shape up, we are going to make you put them hooks on.'"

So, I called back downtown to these people and I told them, and they talked to Melvin and I think Bob and Joe Reichenbach, and they found out that the story was different. So anyway, EEOC ruled in my favor. Of course, Bethlehem Steel filed an appeal. It took a couple of years. I was laid off, I can't remember when because see, I would bump in, I would bump back in, I would go anywhere, because that's where I went to work over at the BOF and stuff. I would bump in because I needed my benefits and stuff for the kids, so I don't really know. I didn't stay out there until they called me. I would come back in.

But anyway, Bethlehem Steel was found guilty, and, of course, they filed their appeal. Now, I never went to any other hearing, and then it came back that they were not guilty, that there was another woman that was in that department who climbed the pole and I could not climb the pole. That was not true, and Bernie Parrish knew that wasn't. She was a black lady, and he knew that was not true. It was two girls were hired off the street for the apprenticeship program. One was a wireman and one was a lineman at the time, and for some reason -- I don't know if they stayed with the company, but I do know that the black girl could not climb the pole, because the guys told me that she didn't. When I went up to the union, I went up to Walter Scott and them and said "Well, tell me what is this name, who is this girl." Nobody could answer -- but you know what I found out later? Bernie Parrish filed a discrimination lawsuit for that girl in the line gang.

This is, like I said, about this separation, which I think has hurt -- started hurting the union, because, like I said, when I would get into areas that the women weren't in, the black men were the ones that helped you the most because they knew what it was like. But it was our union, and other black people aren't going to go against GI Johnson or Bernie Parrish or anything and say "Hey, what do you mean?" you know. I found out a lot of times, Bill, for the average person like me, you don't know and they don't give you help, and that's where I fought the union, because I figured I pay my dues for you to help me. You are kind of like a lawyer to me, and I remember -- I will show you one thing.

When I went to the civil rights conference the first time, there was this guy that got hurt on the job, and he was a maintenance tech and he had taken every test. He worked over -- he was in mobile equipment maintenance, and he had gotten hurt, a tire blew up on him and it fractured his leg and his leg was stiff, he couldn't straighten his one leg, but he could do everything else with some reasonable accommodations. He would have to have maybe a little crane or somebody to come over just give him a hand to put stuff on the table. They wouldn't give him his job back, they wouldn't give him a disability. Now, of course, his lawyer got him a disability, but he wanted to work because he needed the benefits. He was only I think 47 years old, but he had 20 years, I think, 27 years, and he went to people and nobody would do anything, so he came to me, and this was -- I had just came back from a conference on Americans with Disabilities, and so I called their Washington hotline and told them. I said this guy --he has tested. Normally they will say "Oh, she was grandfathered in or he was grandfathered in, he can't do it." This guy tested and passed anything, and he was willing to take anything for them to let him back, and they wouldn't let him back to work.

So, I even went to an attorney downstairs [in the office of Peter G. Angelos, who rented the second floor of the Local 2610 hall for many years] and talked to the attorney down there. Do you know what he told me? "Are you trying to get yourself fired? You are going to get yourself in trouble." I said, "For what?" "Because that guy's attorney told him I can't get your job back, they won't give you disability, it's up to your union."

So, when I called this Americans with Disabilities, the guy told me get a pencil and piece of paper. He said, "You have to write this exact wording that I am telling you," and I wrote the letter exactly like he told me, and we sent it in, and they gave him a disability pension with Bethlehem Steel. So, he got his, and he came and his girlfriend had a surprise retirement party for him, and she called me. She didn't know me or anything, and she asked me if I would come. She said, "Nobody is going to tell him that you are coming," she said, and so I came over, and his mother and father, one of them was in a wheelchair and they cried when they seen me, for helping him, and he was so happy, and I went.

After I retired, I joined the Silhouettes, and the lady working there, you know you start talking, her husband worked at Bethlehem Steel and we were talking, and she knew this guy, and she said "Oh, we're in the same club." She told him, and he sent me a dozen red roses. He's the only one at Bethlehem Steel, that's what he gave me for helping him. I couldn't get over it.

That attorney down there – Peter Angelos, Richard Dickson, whatever his name is--I went to him, Bill, about my hands, about my shoulders, and he would tell me nothing. This guy that worked at my department doing the same job as I did, he went over there and he [the lawyer] told him 'Oh, yeah that's job related' and they filed for -- Peter got "job-related" on carpal tunnel and stuff on his hands, he is telling me that. I went to him the last time before I retired. I went to him because--I can't remember what was going on. Maybe it was when I had my thumb operated on, and he is sitting there and I said, "I don't know why I am I telling you this," and he says, "Why do you say that?" I said, "Because you look like you could just puke." I mean that's what he did. I mean, he was looking at me like disgust, and I told him, I said, "You look like you could just puke."

I hate to use those words, so I got up and I left, and I was off, had to have my shoulders operated on and my hand, and Social Security gave me a disability. I mean I only filed it because I had to. I was out over a year. I think from like in refrigeration, I would have to carry the Freon bottles and everything, and they weighed 30 pounds. I would put them up on my shoulders because it was easier to go up the steps. We had to climb up the steps in the cranes and everything, and then when I got into this new job, which was the best job I loved since I have been down there, but it was hard, everything --Motor Repair. I built the wheel assemblies and stuff for the overhead cranes and the magnets and everything for that, put in new bearings and stuff, but everything was so heavy that a lot of times, we only had the one crane, and if the crane was not -- you know, being held up, I would just take my shoulders like and push stuff over, and I had this shoulder operated on twice and this other one done twice, and I had like some kind of little round thing put in my thumb. My shoulders still bother me, and I haven't worked since 2001, but if Social Security hadn't gave me a disability, I probably would still be down there with my SIP every year or something with this shoulder, but I would have still been working because I would have like to have that 50 grand. Now I don't know what else to say.

One great story—as I got involved in the union, and learned more, I started helping out other workers and I helped one guy get his disability. Then he decided to retire so they had the party for him in the department and he was thanking everyone and saying how much he was going to miss us all, and then he says "I especially want to thank Mary for all of her help," and "she's not afraid of the company" and he said he had a special present for me. So, he gave it to me, right in front of everyone and it was this [she holds up a box with two brass balls in it].

Well, when I first started when I had shift work, I was married and then --yeah, I lived in Essex across from Salvos, and then we bought this house when this development was first built in '71. Moved in here in February '71, and I started at Bethlehem Steel in April of '71. But my kids--when my husband and I broke up, I had six children, I had three by my first marriage, three by my second marriage--when we broke up, my first husband, he could have cared less. He has never ever seen his kids or could care less, we always told him he could, but my second husband loved his children, and I knew I couldn't take care of six kids. I mean, I knew I couldn't, so we agreed that he would take those three, I would keep these, and then in the summer when I had my vacation the children would come up with me for those two weeks, so that went on like that.

But right after him and I broke up, my older boys were getting ready in the teenage years, and he was very strict on them, and, of course, I would come home, and I would go to bed. I mean they would be sitting here, everything would be fine, and I would wake up three o'clock in the morning with the police banging on the door because everybody would be coming into my house because I was asleep and all or I was working, and it was -- I could never go through it again. I mean it was very, very hard times. I mean, I just said the police were out at somebody else's house a couple of weeks ago, and I was out on the porch and I said to the next-door neighbor, I said, "Whew, I can remember the years when they were always here." I said, "Whenever you seen the police, it was here," and then my son, my oldest son committed suicide.

I got laid off in September of '82, and he committed suicide in December 10th of '82, and his girlfriend was pregnant, and my granddaughter was born six months after my son died to the very day, and she just passed away October 23rd. She had cerebral palsy, and she had gotten a cold, and her mother, her mother was so good -- really took good care of her, and she would stay in the room with her when she would get sick, and Mary woke up, she was gasping for breath. She called the paramedics, and they lost her twice before they got her to the hospital, and then at the hospital and she wasn't brain dead because they took her off the respirator, she could breathe, but she had so much brain damage that she would never wake up or have -- she would have to be tube fed and all.

So her poor mother, they told her you know, why we are telling you this, and she said "Yes." Oh, God, Bill, it was awful because she crawled in that bed, she loved that little girl, and I guess it was maybe two hours after that, the doctor came in, he said, "I think the Lord is making the decision for you," because her organs started shutting down, and he told Mary, he said, "By law we have to go there and give her needles" and stuff like that to resuscitate her and Mary said "No," she said she just didn't want to be in there, and they said "Well, it will take a couple of hours." So that's what happened, she passed away October 23rd. But I mean it was like -- now I know why God has you have children when you are young, because if I had them now when you get older, things -- you look at things different.

I mean now, do you think I would put up with that shit at Bethlehem Steel? No way. But at that time, it's like oh, my God, I've got to go to work, I've got to do this, and I mean when my husband left here, he took everything, he took everything. We had a very, very violent relationship, and that's why I got out because it was getting really -- and the only thing --I mean I could take pretty much take care of myself, but I would still get the shit beat out of me, you know, so when we decided to break up, I said look -- I was afraid to come around him. I said "When you move out, I will come back in," and I had my neighbor, I said "Let me know when I can come in," and she said "The moving people were out and the guy, one of the moving men" --because she asked if they wanted some iced tea, it was in the summer, and he said "What that man is doing to that house is a shame."

So, when I called her, she called me when they were gone and I said, "Well, I will have to come back and clean it." She said, "Well, Mary, I'm going to tell you it's not going to be hard because he took everything." He took switches off the light switch to be nasty, took my stove, my refrigerator, and I said "Well, what's the sense," I couldn't get upset or anything because there wasn't anything I could do, but I went to take a bath and there wasn't any hot water, and I said "If I go downstairs and he took the furnace, I'm really going to be pissed." What it was, when they took the stove, they had to cut the gas off, so I didn't have hot water for the heater, but I made it.

Like I was just talking to my daughter yesterday, because she's living in Las Vegas, and I didn't try to get her down to the Point because I know how dangerous it was down there. I especially think now, with more young girls because they are really -- I knew some of these young girls would come in that they just hired and they would have them feeding out there on those lines, and when I got there, those men had to have fifteen years or something to get on those lines.

I mean. I can remember a girl coming in there crying because she was scared to death. She wanted to work, she was willing to do anything, but she didn't like that because it scared her to death. I didn't push my daughter, but I was telling her come on, Stace, you know she was driving a limo, she was driving a cab. I said, "Everybody has got to work." I said, "You are going to find very, very few people that like what they do." I said, "I knew I had to work, and I was going to work where the money was," and I said, "And look, I've got a good pension, I have good Social Security, I can do what I want." I would like more. I lost $300 when they did that [declared bankruptcy] and the benefits, but I said, "Some women I know live on $800 a month," and that's what I tell my daughters-in-law and all them. I can remember when I would be working, because I was young like everybody else and we would stop on North Point Road, and sometimes instead of going home, we would go for breakfast and go to work. Now that would kill you, but I can remember some of my friends would be laughing because they didn't work, they would laugh at me "Ha-ha, you've got to go to work," but whose got the last laugh now? And when you are old, I don't know what I would do at this age not being able to have anything that I enjoy.

Well, I got involved in the union through Sandy Wright, because when things would happen to me over in refrigeration, I think it was in '91 or '93. I had been there, yeah, 20 years. I started in '71 years, so I had been there about 20 years. Sandy is a very, very smart girl! When I would go through these things, guys would take me, "Mary, do you know Sandy Wright? Go talk to Sandy Wright." Well, it was again that "I'm going to take care of myself," you know, and I could be used as long as they are not the only one being treated bad, but anyway, Dave Wilson was married to Sandy's cousin, Dee. She was very involved in the union.

Well, see, I started working with Dee, and that's why Dee and I got along really good because Dee and I, we worked over in the tin mill, and Dee knew I worked, worked hard and we worked on pulling scrap and all that, but Marie Wilson, that's who Dave was married to, Marianne Wilson. Anyway, Jimmy Harmon came back and gave me -- it was at a conference in Atlantic City, a civil rights conference, and he gave me the little brochures and all that, and it had about the last Women of Steel.

So, Sandy and I decided we would go up and talk to Dave and he said "Yeah." We wanted to go, so it was me and Sandy and it was a black lady, I can't remember her name, she lived on Elwood, she worked at one of the other places that shut down, and a lady from 2609. We went up to Boston, Cape Cod or somewhere up that way, and that was the first that I had ever --I had never heard of CLUW [The Coalition of Labor Union Women], never ever heard of CLUW, and I thought the CLUW was more -- I liked it better for the women.

Up to this time, in 2610, no women were active in the union. Like I said 2609 is a whole different ball game, whole different ball game than 2610. No, not that I know of. I think maybe Sue Guido, but I never even knew she was any of this until when I went over there, there were papers laying around. The civil rights committee used to be about fifteen people, and that's where I seen her, but so far as ever any other woman,

So Dave Wilson gave me the opportunity to go, and I went to that conference there in Boston I think it was, Massachusetts somewhere, and then we went to a convention in Las Vegas, and I think that was in '93, and I was elected as a delegate for the steelworkers from the District 8, because I think it was like three of us, three delegates, and I mean they had the vice-president -- yeah, I don't know, I was elected delegate. So, every  time anything involved CLUW, I was to go, and I was chairman of their women and nontraditional jobs committee, and we put on a lot of things. One of our conventions out -- the last one I went to in Las Vegas we had -- remember What's My Line? It was me and it was two other girls, and we were dressed like hard hats and stuff like that. Instead of having the audience ask me, because it would be too hard, we had about five people behind us and the job description was -- I think it was my job -- no, it wasn't my job, it was another girl's job, I can't remember.

But anyway, they were asking us -- no, it was my job and they were asking questions and then they voted. I don't think anybody got it right, because then we had to stand up and say it, and the one girl was a baggage handler and the other girl was a communication worker, I think it was, but we were describing the job, what you would do on my job. Once we went to Philadelphia, we had a workshop where we had Karen -- I forget Karen's last name. She was an electrician, and we made little switches and stuff like that, and they told women how to make the telephones, move their jacks and things like that, and it was nice.

Women in other industries were having the same problems. Yes, very much, and especially some of the new trades where the women started getting into, some of the building trades, and a lot of it was the same stuff. You know people feel sorry for you and all, but people don't like to stand up. There's very few that want to -- they see what you are going through, and they don't want to put themselves through it, and I never blamed anybody for that because I knew it, I knew.

When I was in refrigeration, almost every damn day, I would either cry at work or cry coming home, and I would say to Bob Arrowwood, "I shouldn't have to do this." I would go to my superintendent, and I remember one time with the shop steward, I went over there and I laid my head down, and I don't cuss, but I came out with some very, very foul language, laid my head, I was just sobbing. I said, "You have got to do something with that blankety blankety foreman." I mean, they knew what he was doing to me, and the shop steward was there, and I remember the one that -- you know how you keep getting elected and elected, and the only time you see them is election time? He was very well aware, but one of the new shop stewards one time--the older one was on vacation and this guy from electrical construction came, and I forget what the problem was at that time, but when he went in there, the foreman starts talking awful about me to him, and he said, "Wait a minute, wait a minute, I'm her union rep, do you realize what you are saying to me?" But he had gotten away with it. That was Larry Burke. He only -- I only think he ran that one time because nobody did anything, Bill. It's unfortunate to say, but they didn't. It was like "If I tell you what your rights are, I've got to work and do my job," and that's sad, it's really sad.

I tried to get women involved in the Women of Steel. I don't know if I turn people off, I really don't, because I would take stuff all around. I just don't know why I couldn't get the women involved. I got Flo Jones. I'm the one who got Flo, and I took -- I see Gail Fleming, she was in the paper where she is going to CLUW and stuff now. I got Gail and all. Now Flo did things. Gail was pretty much ready to get out of work, but I mean - and then see, too, Bill, a lot of times women -- I could do what I did in the later years because I didn't have a husband. A lot of husbands just aren't understanding, and now I'm sure it's got to be harder because how can you buy a house? I know my son and his wife, they are both working, and I mean he's got enough problems. I'm sure if she came home crying all the time, he would be "Quit the damn job and go somewhere else," so that creates a problem.

I just wish that there would be something that if somebody had a problem like that, people that knew what it was like could go to somebody -- I don't know if it would be like an attorney or if it would be an arbitrator or what, or who. I mean, I don't know how to explain it, to help them, because you shouldn't have to work like that. Luckily we didn't have outhouses emptied on us and stuff like that, but I mean, when the girls went to the coke ovens, there were many a girl could tell you, they come around the corner and the guy was going to the bathroom, because a lot of times they really forgot, too, that the women worked there.

I remember one in the coal fields, a lot of the girls worked in the coal fields, and I remember this one girl, she was so funny, and our bathroom in the coke oven had been a men's bathroom, so when we came there, they had it divided in half. Well, OSHA came down because it only had two doors. Now it was just one and one, so they had to make a door in the back, and it was months and months, you know, we had the holes knocked out, you had the tarp laying down. I remember this girl Libby, she went -- everybody would take their clothes in the shower with them because they had the one big shower, and Libby says, "I'm not taking my clothes in there anymore." She said, "If they haven't seen a woman by now, tough shit," but it was so funny because when we first moved in, they didn't brick it all the way to the top, and we caught the guys looking in there. It was hysterical because it was like school kids, and then we had windows and there was no air conditioner or anything, so in the summer we would open the windows and we were across from Kohl Chemical, and that was a couple stories high, and after a while some of us happened to notice there's all these men standing on the railing, they could look right into the bathrooms, so it was funny. And this girl Libby after we discovered that, they had a men's bathroom down in the coal field, so that the girls went over on this belt line and they were standing up there. Well, you should have heard the stink from those men because the women when they caught -- then the woman started "Ha ha," and it was hysterical because when it was us, it was like "Oh, God, guys will be guys," but with them, it was a whole different story. It was funny, and I worked on the belt lines like how that girl did in there.

    I liked the movie *North Country* because one of the girls on my committee was a miner, her name was Bonnie something, but she was from, I think, Pennsylvania, the mines there. I think she got involved in the union kind of to get out of that, because she would tell us some of the stories that happened in the bathrooms and stuff, and she didn't really come to that many meetings after I became involved, because a lot of places were small and it cost -- when they have these conventions, except for Vegas, these hotels are outrageous, the prices and all, but I knew -- I mean if they had the women in the building trades, you are going to find the same thing.

    But now they have a young girl that was in electrical construction. Now I talked to her -- I asked if she had any trouble with any of the men, she never said anything, and I asked her, and it was because they hired a girl in electrical construction, they hired an ironworker and they hired a maintenance tech, and the ironworker, she could pretty much I think  take care of herself. Because I had said something to the little girl, the electrician, and she had met her like when they went on the stadiums or different jobs for the locals before they got hired there. She said "Oh, Priscilla can take care of herself," but Priscilla ended up I think, drinking or doing drugs or something and not showing up and she ended up losing her job. But Sandy -- I never heard any of the guys say anything bad about her. They said that she was really a good worker, and she could work harder than some of the men. She was a very tiny small girl, but she never ever said she had any problems, and it didn't seem like over there -- but see, with her it was at this time she was about the same age as the new men coming in, and they all were learning and she knew what she was doing, so I think it was a little different than us women being -- I was like 31 when I started being thrown in there with people that didn't want you there and weren't going to show you, because that's how they treated the black men, they wouldn't show them anything. So, I think it's a little different, because the other girl, the maintenance tech, I think she could pretty much take care of herself, and she never really complained about it either.

I said I just finished watching that *North Country*. I said "Boy, am I glad he [Bill Barry] is not here to do the interview because it sure has got me pissed off." I said it brought back memories, and I mean I always cry at some of the stuff because I can remember one time, and my problem was my father and my mother, they didn't have much of an education. My father was a truck driver. They had seven kids, and my father always taught us and all my kids, "Whatever you do, go out and work, don't ask nobody for nothing, don't take nothing from anybody you don't know," so that is how I always wanted to work, and I always -- if I couldn't do the heaviest kind of stuff, I tried to say "Well, I will pick up this for you and even it out," and it was just so hard for me to see that this didn't make a shit, they did not care and I'm talking about superintendents.

I went over about this Mr. Hooth, and the superintendent I had now was gone, and I mean I was crying so bad that snot flew out of my nose, that's how upset I was. You know what he said to me? "Get out of here, get out of here and get control of yourself." And I mean it was like -- you know what I mean? It was just awful, awful.

And, like I said, would it be different now? But you see that's how supervision felt for us then. I mean not all of them did, but now it's like that's how all companies are feeling about their people. You don't care.

My son was a supervisor, operation superintendent over at Medical Waste over on the other side of the Key Bridge, and this one guy was really having financial problems, and he came to my son, and, of course, my son was a maintenance guy, and he went to the big boss who would have had to okay it. The guy wanted his vacation, his money and not take the vacation, and Michael said here this guy said -- it wasn't that he was asking for a loan. He said, "Mom, he couldn't have cared less, he didn't care about what that guy wanted or anything," no. Then everybody would want to do it, but see my son, he couldn't -- he drives a truck because he couldn't be -- my son got in trouble and he was in prison and he was sentenced to seven years, but he served like three years, and he was married and he bought a house in Dundalk, and what it was he was stone drunk. I had been down his house that morning, I was going to a union meeting, and he worked up in Cockeysville for Maryland Specialty Wire. He was on the 11:00 to 7:00 shift and he had just gotten home, and I came over there and I said, "Come on, Mike, let's go out and get something to eat for breakfast. I want to go to the union meeting later," and he said, "Oh mom, I'm so tired," because he had worked the 3:00 to 7:00 and the 11:00 to 7:00, and so I said okay.

So I'm getting ready to go, and I'm not one of these mothers that it's this other guy's fault, but this guy was from the neighborhood, and whenever the shit would always go downhill, he was always in the middle of, but he never got in any trouble, but he was always the one like this. So, he came over and he said to Mike, "Come on, let's go out and drink." So, they go out and they drink, they got plastered and they got in a fight with two guys, and my son goes away to jail because he had been in trouble as a juvenile.

So anyway in order to come out, they try to see if he got a job program and all, and this Dave Fenwick, who was in refrigeration, the only guy that stood up for me, he's dead now, he said to me, "Mary, I've got a friend that works at the one Medical Waste that was a steelworker. He said he would hire Mike."

So, Mike got out and he went over there and went to work. Well, he was such a good worker. He belonged to -- it was BFI and they had what they call a chairman's club, and the first year he worked there, he was named to the chairman's club-- here's what it is. Only five people or something out of this company. But anyway, he got all these pictures. This is how many people were up and only five were chosen and he was chosen the first year. But he couldn't do it, because he was brought up by work, and he was a supervisor and he would tell the guys to do something and they would say they didn't know, and instead of Michael saying "okay, here, give me the wrench" -- he would go to the job, and after a while they seen that, and then the company, too, whenever these the incinerators would have to be relined, he would have to stay there around the clock because you would have to turn up so many degrees. It just got so he couldn't take it because then they started hiring people that didn't want to work, who would bring their kids there in this medical waste place, said they couldn't get a babysitter, and he just started drinking, so he said he had to get away. So he got his own truck and he says he is better like that, but he made good money, but he just couldn't handle that. But that's the story of my life, all these things.

I went out in 2001, I had my shoulder operated. I officially retired, I think it was May of 2003. Right before the end. Well, see, I wasn't there, I didn't even go back for my retirement or anything because I had been off for two years with my shoulders. I went to those meetings, and I mean I retired -- well, when I got the disability at Bethlehem Steel, I had to pay them money back because they were paying me sick money, so that's when I talked to Jim Huber, and he asked me how much time I had and he didn't know. I don't think he knew all this was going to come down then either, you know. I had 31 and a half years, so I thought I was getting $1,800 a month pension and $1,500 in Social Security, boy, this is great. I thought "Well, yeah, they are paying my medical," and that's how come I retired. If I had known that the bucket was going to fall out, I would have tried to go back to work and said "God, please can't you say I tried again" or something.

I don't regret leaving because I lived for that day. I hated getting up, and I wanted to work the daylight, so I had to sacrifice getting up, but I always said, "I don't care if I don't do anything, it's better than being there." I don't care, because since I have been out of there, I haven't had a cold, and I was getting lung infections. The last year I was at the hospital all the time because I couldn't breathe. They would have to give me those treatments where I would have to breathe that mist in and everything. Since I have been out of there, I haven't had that, but I have lung problems from there, but I haven't had colds and all like I was getting.

After the bankruptcy, I lost $300 and some dollars a month. Plus, my insurance. I had kept my insurance, I was paying -- it went from $84 to $534 a month, so I paid that because I always had Blue Cross and I always liked it and I wasn't 65 yet. So then when we got the government help, I only had to pay $187. So, because I went out on disability, my disability -- I got Medicare earlier than I would have. I think I got it when I was 64, because I think you have to be out two years or something, so when I got that, then I lost the other, so my insurance went up to $295 a month, which I still paid. And then come December I got a letter that the insurance was going up again, so I called, and it went up to $428, and I said "Well, enough is enough." So that's when I went and I got the Medigap Blue Cross Blue Shield Maryland, it's $143 a month I think it is. And the rest of us are on Medicare.

Would I have wanted my kids to work there? It would depend on -- my daughters, I would have to know where they were going to go to work, because on the steel side -- my daughters are frilly frilly, you know, but she's got a mouth. She probably could because she's strong, stronger than what she appears to be, but it's dangerous. My one son by my second husband, he was going to go there, was going to work during the summer. He's a design engineer for Nissan up in Detroit, and he was going to work there during the summer, but he was still in college and he was getting ready to graduate, and he had a hernia so he couldn't. Had to get that operated on while he was still under his dad's insurance, and I'm kind of glad because he is such a smart boy. If something would have happened to him, it would have been terrible, but I was so glad. But Carolyn Holt -- do you remember her?--she was president of Local 9116 at first. That covered your clerks and your expediters, more or less the people that worked in the office. I mean they were out in the mills, the expediters and stuff, so it wasn't like in production.

She was a pistol. She was really a good union officer, probably the first woman, who was an officer, right after they won that lawsuit because they found out that the men and the women were doing the same thing and they were paying the men a lot more money for the same thing. That was in I think the '80s, you know, so that's what I'm saying. When I seen this movie [*North Country*], it was like, I bet you could go to any apprenticeship place or any job site that's got the women and I'm sure they have stories, too.

I don't know what the future of the plant is. I know that when I talked to the guys, they made more money than they have ever made, and at first the profit sharing and everything, they got the profit-sharing checks. I do think that a big part of their problem was management. I mean they had five bosses for four workers, and they were all relatives, and the stealing, I mean, come on. You've got to be a moron. See people would report, nothing would be done, but that's the only thing that makes me angry is that the salary people got more benefits than we did, and they are the reason that the place has went under. I don't know. I don't like all these foreign countries taking over our manufacturing.

Like my son and I were talking or my daughter, I said "Let me see if I know some unions out there in Vegas, maybe you can get into something," and she said, "Mom, out here in Vegas, believe me if you want to work, you are going to work." She said that's the place for the jobs, but the traffic is just -- it's just boomed, and she said "You don't want to work in Vegas if you don't have a job" she said because there are jobs, but she said there's not manufacturing but the housing industry and all that. But one thing I seen out there -- now they have to go get health certificates, they have to apply -- they have to go through all kinds of stuff to get a job as a waitress, and when

I was out at my friend Mike's house last year, I was flipping through the TV and the local channel, it had people who were denied this -- whatever this permit is to work. You have to be checked for hepatitis. I imagine that's probably just in the food handling, but all of these things, and my daughter told me now it's really bad because they go back ten years on your employment, plus they are checking all your credit. If you've got bad credit, they are not hiring you, and I mean I look at the kids nowadays--half of them don't know the stuff that I can just still remember from school let alone what I forgot. I can't understand what's going on, where are they going to get these jobs.

Now I play bingo. I win big sometimes, most of the time. I don't know. Playing 36 cards at a time. I always played bingo. I played bingo -- well, my oldest son would be 46 this year, and I started playing bingo before he was born, and then I could only go once a week, and, of course, when I worked, I couldn't go except on the weekends. I started like over in Towson down in that area, and I would go wherever I was living, but now I go down in Dundalk, but with Las Vegas, see I always saved -- I would always have $200 every month taken out of my pay and put in my Christmas club, and I still do that, and that's the only money that I take when I go to gamble. I mean I would like to take $5,000 or something. I have it to take, but no, I'm not going to.

That's my friend Mike, he moved to Vegas, he will be 82 in August, and he came back, he's got a sister here and she's got Alzheimer's, and when I went out last October and came back in November, he came back with me. He was going to stay between my house, her house and his nieces and nephews, and by the end of December, I had to get on the Internet and get him a ticket back. He went back January the 6th, said he couldn't stand it, it's too boring, and I mean he's on a fixed income, he doesn't have a lot of money, but he goes twice a day. He knows when they have -- sometimes they pay triple pay and he goes on them, and then they have like these hot balls. When the hot ball gets to 4 or $5,000, you go there, and they cater to them, they cater to the natives out there, and like he gets three free nights at the hotel and a slot tournament free, and he lives there, so he just goes on down, and I like it out there.

I'm hoping, because I'm a person that I have to have the air conditioner on because I really don't know -- but I say, "What do I do?" I go from my air-conditioned house to my air-conditioned car to the air-conditioned casino. I just decided that it's a big move for me really because my family is here, I love my doctor, and those are the things that really have me asking— "is this really what you want to do?"

My son, you know, I have one child here in Maryland, he lives in Conowingo, and he told me "Mom, if that's what you want to do, you always like to go out there, go." And my other kids, they said "Don't save no house for us, go and enjoy yourself," and I think if I've got 20 years, hey, I'm really going to be lucky, why not go where I enjoy myself?

I can't describe working at The Point -- I mean it was interesting. It had its good times, it had its sad times, but overall, I think other than that specific area, I can't say. And the girls, you know. It was so much fun when they had all the women, when they had the coke ovens, it was so much fun to see all the women down there working in the coal field. Those girls would come in from these coal fields and we all wore long underwear and then you had your dungarees, and then you had those uniforms on, but they had to do that because the cold gusts and they would come in like that, and their backs would be soot and they would have to wash each other's back and stuff because you couldn't get all that soot. I can remember when we would walk out, they had the quencher, and when you first went there, because I ruined some clothes until I realized you walk out and they would quench that coat and make it cold with water, and it would have these little black dots. Now if you didn't touch them and they dried, they would blow off, but at first you go like this [brushes off her shirt], and it was all streaks and it wouldn't come out.

And they used to have a restaurant down there, and it was nice, it was nice. I mean I didn't like swing shift, but when I went into the labor gang and it wasn't the best of money, and then I was just sweeping in the machine shop, I think they call it, the coke ovens down there in the maintenance shop and that was pretty nice. Most of the time I was the only girl around. So when I went to refrigeration, the guy at the employment office said that was the best job but the worst boss. He is deceased now, his name was Larry Reece, he would holler at you, but if anybody else said anything about his workers, he would jump on them like I don't know what. Always took up for his workers. We were working over one of the hot strip mills, and the mechanic asked me to go back and get his lunch because it was lunchtime, and he says "Pick me up a Coke at Servomation," so I'm driving the truck, I'm coming down to go back to the job, and the boss pulls up, I'm stopped, and he says, "Where have you been?" I said, "I went up to Servomation, got a Coke." He said, "If I ever catch your ass driving that truck anywhere else" -- and when I went back and told the guy, he said, "Mary, he don't mean anything by it." He said, "That's how he is," and like the next day Reece says to me, "Hey, Mary, grab that truck and go up to Servomation, and get me a Coke" -- he let me know, and that's how he was.

But one time in the summer, comfort cooling always came last as far as refrigeration. In this one mill, the office kept calling up, their air conditioner was making noise, it was cold, but they said it kept making noise and all. After about the fourth call, Reece, goes out, gets in his car, drives over there, walks in the office, turns it off, said, "Ain't making any noise now; is it? Out he goes, but he passed away, but that's what everybody said, "You didn't dare say anything to him about his employees," but the ones that took over after him they talk about their employees like dogs, but he always took up for his men.

The only thing, yes, that I do regret is, like I said, most of the time I worked down there, I worked with all men, I was the only girl and I had a lot of good friends, but when I retired, that's the bad part about--it is all my friends were men. Their wives don't want you to come over, and a lot of them even when you see them it's like "hi," and of course I know how, and that's the only bad thing because I don't really have--I never really formed good relationships with women. I always did get along better with men.

I did volunteer work for my doctor for a while, and her little receptionist was getting married, and that's why she wanted me in there so I could fill in for the two weeks where she was on her honeymoon. Well, I know how she's young, she was excited about her wedding and all, and I said to my mom I'm not interested in that shit. I said, "If they talk about putting a coupling on that got stuck or something like this, good," but women can't understand. But that's the only thing I regret, because like I said I don't have friends-- like my friend Mike, I met him at the bingo hall, and we started traveling together because you had to pay single supplement. He had asked me would I mind sharing a room. I said I work with all guys, it didn't bother me. I will flip you over across that room if you bug me, but we have been friends, but we couldn't live together. I wish we could, because he bought a doublewide mobile that's bigger than this house, it's longer, way longer than here, and it's too big. He wanted to sell it to me, but he wants to sell it too much, because he got all new carpet and all and all the furniture, and I don't like his furniture. It's beautiful, but it's not me with my dog.

But I said I wish him and I could live together because it would be so much cheaper, but we are like Felix and Alex, I walk in a room, and I don't know what I do, I don't have to do nothing but I've got it torn up. I had a friend who just passed away two years ago, she was 49. She was over in the hospice, and I was over there visiting her, and I'm sitting there and after a while I said, "Bec?" She said, "Yeah?" I said, "What have I been doing?" She said, "What have you been doing? Nothing." I said, "I know. Why do I have this area tore up."? I mean I did, I had Kleenexes here and books. I mean I don't know why I'm like that, and that's how -- when I go to his place, when I go to Vegas, I will stay with him for a while, but I always go to the hotels two or three times. I can't stay the whole month with him because I have to go in my room and keep the door shut, I can't open the door, and I make my bed as soon as I get up, but it's not to his perfection.

The only one I usually keep in touch with is Flo and Francis Almond. Another lady Kitty, she retired before I did. Her husband worked there, he retired so she had to retire.

LeRoy McClelland, Sr.
May, 2006

It's LeRoy, L-e-R-O-Y. [emphasis on second syllable] Well, even on my birth certificate--I didn't realize that until so many years later--that I was a LeRoy and not a Leroy. A little quirk.

Well, where I grew up was in Baltimore City. It was right at 115 South Collington Avenue, and them homes down there at that time--probably still is, I haven't been back there for a long time--but they are like a city block long. We had from the street of Collington Avenue, behind us was Madeira, which was the alleyway, and when we grew up, I guess a lot had to do with the sort of the group that stuck together there. We did a lot of playing over in Patterson Park, Cannon Hill and Baby Pond and used to be a diving pool that we would swim in on the weekends. What I remember more outstanding is that we never had a refrigerator. We had an ice box. We never had indoor plumbing. We had outdoor plumbing and growing up with that kind of an atmosphere and to see it change as we got older, was fascinating enough. We had the ice delivered -- would you believe when I tell you this--that we had ice delivered by the horse and wagon, which was really something different and even when they come to collect like rags and newspapers and what have you, it would be horse and wagon. Our vegetables and fruits, it would be horse and wagon. I guess the fascinating part of all of that was in the evening, there would be a guy with a ladder on his shoulder who would light the lights, which were gas-operated lights.

This is part of -- as I was growing up and as these things were going on around us, now where I'm at today at my age 69 thinking back then how uncomplicated things were, how dependent you were on knowing what you knew, not a computer which you stick your hands into and then you ask for a question to be answered. You had those answers because you dealt with people one-on-one, and it was all part of the closeness of neighborhood living compared to what it is today, because today it's fast -- everybody is on a fast track, nobody has got time to even touch a table and feel what the table is. It gets to a point to where you are looking at a part of transition in life that went from uncomplicated, you knew what you had to do, you earned your allowance, there was no "give me," you earned it or you didn't get it. Today, that's changed immensely in a lot of ways. But me, at my age as it is now and where I have already been in the past, I felt there was a lot more that I should be entitled to.

Here I worked 42 years at Sparrows Point. I served our country in the Navy from 1955 to 1959, and you look for certain perks that you were sort of guaranteed would be available, and then because of bureaucracy and funding and all this other thing, these things started to deteriorate. I know I'm jumping round a little bit here, but this is as it's flowing to me is the way it's happening. In the service, I sit back thinking when I come out -- of course I was one of the lucky ones among others who come back in the country with all their arms and limbs and their sensible thinking and mind where others lost their lives. I left buddies who lost their lives over there protecting what we feel to be our liberty and our rights of this country, which now seems to be taking a turn again in wars that we shouldn't even be involved in. We should let people solve their own problems over there and take care of our problems, and our problems basically here are immense. It's health coverage, it's housing, it's so many things.

More importantly, outsourcing. Where is the younger generation - where in the world are they going to find jobs, because everything you look out there is technically operated? There is no hands-on type of operation any more. Everything is computerized. You don't have the education, if you don't have a background of some education from colleges --with me, it was high school, that's all you really needed because that was the commonsense education level we lived in.

Anyway, to get back to another part of where I was at. Come out of the Navy in 1959. We had people from Glenn L. Martin. I don't know how familiar any of you out there would be with that, but in Glenn L. Martin's, they had the P-6M Skymaster, which was a jet-operated sea plane, and we were mechanics on that particular engine. When we were honorably discharged, we had these people come down and solicit us, around fifteen of us who were very qualified in reciprocating engines and jet engines, because that was another fascinating part of life.

We all ended up going out there, went to work for a while with them, and then suddenly the Navy cancels the contract. They cancel the contract, here we are without a job, nowhere to go. So, I went ahead and we put applications in at the fire department, police department, anywhere and everywhere. Bethlehem Steel was one of the big key places at the time because of the money. I mean the money motivates you. So as time went on, I finally get a telegram telling me to report to the employment office of Sparrows Point.

Well, in 1959 I went to Sparrows Point. There were umpteen guys there looking for employment and there were different places that we were not familiar with within the steel mill that would shock you to no end when you first experienced the atmosphere of the steel mill. I, for one, was one that was lucky enough to get a tractor job, but back then I was only 21 years old and I'm saying "tractor." Well, that puts me in mind of the big wheel and the little wheel farmer tractor, I thought that's what they were talking about. So, when they finally get all their health and physicals and all that done and out of the way, they took a group of us over into the tin mill, into the tractor department, and when I walked in there, I'm seeing mechanics working on tractors.

Never recognized those type of things in my life. They were huge and they had big flat wheels, not rubber tires, but big flat wheels-- not flat, flat wheels, but it wasn't air tires but solid rubber tires, and then after we sat there and they introduced each other and then they went ahead and said "this is what you are going to be trained on" and "this is what you are going to do." I'm sitting in the class there, and I'm looking at a couple of people and I'm saying "Hey, let me ask a question, Where is the big tractor with the big wheels and the little wheels, the farm tractor," and the guy looked at me and says, "Hey pal, you are in the steel mill. You are not out on a farm," and it was just like "What?"

And then they went ahead and broke us off into groups, and I went into the tin mill to see the operations of the tractors, and it was -- man, I will tell you when I walked in that door, humongous doors that opened up when you walked in, and I looked around, it was just unbelievable. It took your breath away. It was scary, because you had cranes up there moving back and forth with loads on it, rolls and stuff going back and forth. Tractors driving up and down on the mill floors. People that seemed to be walking from one area to other, just sort of like a timing type of thing where you knew to be here because the tractor was over here and that kind of thing.

My first training was on a 16,000-pound single boom tractor, which means that you pick up one coil, a 16,000-pound coil, and you would take it from a bay and you would put it on unit. You would feed it into the unit, they would process it. You would go on the other side of it, take that coil off and take it on down to what was known as coil pack and somebody would band it at the other end.

In fact, all that was done here was tape. It wasn't steel bands, unless it was oil plate, something that wouldn't hold the tape. They would put a piece of tape on it, and you would take it down to the coil pack or if it had a defect in it, you would take what was called the skin pass or the tin mill grave yards, which was products that they couldn't send to that customer but may accommodate some other customer, and if it didn't, then—

The tin was used for appliances and automobiles and even bobby pins in some cases. They were used for toys. They were used for food containers, battery brackets and all kinds of usage. As time went on, they got into different type of plating. They went into galvanizing, they went into oil plate. They went into chrome plate. DNI steel, what we used to call skinny plate, and the reason why it was all brought on was because of competition from aluminum.

The galvanized would be used for trash bins and storage and sheds and awnings. The oil plate was usually used when you are sending that product overseas to keep it from rusting. That was the basic part of oil plating. They made oil filters. In fact, Prince Albert tobacco cans was one of their products also. I mean the metal was, not the making of the container. That was done by the consumer.

The skinny plate was a real thin material that they used for filters, used them like the screening that you would find in your furnace filter or you would see like the little fence -- not a fence, but a little screen type of thing. They were used for that kind of product. Me personally, I can't speak for others, but the fascinating part in the steel mill was the way things operated was one person depended on the other to be here and do this. You got such a close camaraderie with the group that you worked with, it was like a second family when you were in there, and you had certain jobs that you were assigned. I went from a 16,000-pound tractor to a 20,000-pound tractor, which was a split boom tractor that would pick up a 20,000-pound or two 10,000-pound coils. Prep line, we would feed the prep line, take off the prep line, you would feed skin mills, take off the skin mills.

The tractor operators never got off to feed the mill. Back then you didn't do any of that. What you had was feeders on the prep lines, you had operators on the prep lines. You had catchers on the prep line. All the tractor service did was service that particular line. The shears down on the shear floor, they would have shear tractors that would take off the square pieces of steel that were box steel is what they used to make lids, canned lids, stuff like that from, but you would have a crane feed those shear operations. Down on the plating lines, you would have a tractor feed it on one end and then on the other side of the building, you would have a tractor take off, and in between that you would have a girl, which was known as the CDR girl, who would inspect that steel inch by inch as it rolled right in front of her so she could pick up any defect. Just like the girls on the shear floor and the girls in the tin house, which was called flippers back then, they would take individual sheets, squares of sheet and flip it one at a time to be sure before the product left the Point was quality.

That was one of the main things down there was quality, and in fact, it was like when you entered into that steel mill, it was like entering into a closed world and nothing else outside them walls existed--just what was happening in that mill. You took pride in what you were doing, and I know I did, and many times we would stop off up on North Point Road just to talk about the day that we had and the competition between the other crews we had. So it was a competitiveness there that we put on ourselves because we were proud and still proud to this very day of being steelworkers, and I guess the bigger part of all that came with change where I -- for one I'm a little ahead of myself.

I, for one, when I first went into the mill, I'm looking where the bathrooms were and I was shocked to see that there was black, which was colored, and white, two separate facilities, and there was one water fountain between them. I couldn't rationale what this meant, it just took me by surprise, and I would sit waiting to service one of the units and I would see a guy come out -- black guy come out of the colored section there and drink water. I would see a guy, a white guy come out and drink water out of the same fountain. So, I said to the operator, I said, "What the hell is that all about over there?" He said, "LeRoy, that's been here since time." I said, "Well, I hear that, but why now?" I mean this is the '50s. We are almost into the '60's, I don't understand this

And that's the part I'm trying to tell you. When I went in the service, black, white, we all were recruited together. I ended up going to Bainbridge [in Port Deposit, MD] for basic training, which was a 14-week basic training, black, white, again from all over the country. I mean you name the state, there was somebody there from that state, white, black, Latino, Chinese, whatever, they were Americans. So anyway, we went through all that training and all, and none of that existed within the service. I left Bainbridge and went to Norman, Oklahoma, which was A & P school for aviation, and there were blacks in the same routine, and you never saw or felt any of that separation.

The only experience we had -- in Norman, Oklahoma, you never had that phase of what we would call blatant discrimination. Wherever we went to eat, we all ate together. But in Norfolk, Virginia, it was a total different turn and that was a surprise. We left Norman, Oklahoma, went to Memphis, Tennessee, for A school. From there we went to Norfolk, Virginia, waiting transportation, in my case to Gitmo Bay, Guantanamo Bay back then. So, we want to go in town because we had a weekend liberty here, we were going to go in town, and when we went in town we seen these signs, "Dogs and sailors, stay off the lawn," and I couldn't understand what that was about. I'm looking at the guy and said, "Look at this shit," we are over here, going out to protect this country and they don't even want us walking on their grass. This is Norfolk, Virginia.

So that being a bit of the conversation, we go to go in the restaurant, and we had a couple of black guys that were with us that were in our crew, so we go in. The guy -- first thing he does is run up in front of us and says, "Hey, you guys can't come in here. Youse can."

I said, "Say that again." "The black guy, the three black guys can't come in here." I said, "What do you mean they can't come in here? They are sailors, they are military people. They are serving this country, they are protecting your ass. What do you mean they can't come in here?"

He said, "Look, guys, this is the way it is here. You are welcome, but they are not," and we just took one look at him and said, "Well, we will tell you what, we're not either." We all walk out confused, but we should have listened to the captain of the base because he said we would not be sort of accepted in a mixed group.

This was absolutely a huge jump from my community around Patterson Park. That was another thing we can never face and learn is discrimination sort of crept into us. I went to elementary, went to all the schools. There were black, there were white. Nobody ever, ever dwelled on this fact of differences. As I think about it now, I think because back then they sort of separated themselves. They just sort of had this thing. There was the Polish neighborhoods and there was Italian neighborhoods, and there were Irish neighborhoods and there were black neighborhoods, they sort of done that on their own, so you never put a lot of emphasis on it. When we went to the park, you didn't see many blacks there by the way and that was by their own choosing, but that wasn't because anybody back then discriminated and said, "We don't want you here." You go to school, they were at school.

Maybe not as many as it was before as it is today because they had their own schools, they did their own thing. So, I guess what I'm driving at here is a lot of this was brought on because of their own will and their own wants, not something that they were forbidden to do.

Yes, but we did have what they used to call a Jim Crow car, which was understood, I mean, there was never an argument. The person, the black person would get on the street car, they would go in the back, bingo, automatically. There was no disputing about it or arguing about it. It was an accepted way of life. I think a lot of that for guys my age who were brought under that kind of style of living never took much seriousness about the discrimination, because I guess -- I don't know how else to explain it. We didn't really accept that because there was no objecting with black, white, German, Chinese, whatever, but we did and we were proud of our neighborhoods, the Polish neighborhood and the Irish neighborhoods and the Italian neighborhoods and the black neighborhoods. They were all proud people in their own ways, I guess.

I remember my father and neighbor sitting out on the steps with a jar of beer. They would send down to get beer –sometimes I was sent down to get it but if it wouldn't be for the bartender saying come in the side door, we wouldn't have been able to do that, but at times we did. My God. This was on Pratt Street, it was right on Pratt and Bellington. I don't remember the name of it, it's so far back. That would only be on weekends. It would never be during the week. It would be on the weekends, and that -- Christ, when we were kids, we would play games called Tin Can Willy, we played red line and cowboys, Indians and cowboys and stuff like that, and played ball.

Patterson Park, Highlandtown--because the main operations here, besides Sparrows Point, was the ship yard, too, and General Motors, and naturally at that time, too, Glenn L. Martin, so it was a real mix of workers in that area.

My dad worked at General Motors. In fact, my brother followed in his footsteps. Me, I was the only one who started off in Bethlehem Steel against will of my father who said that's the most dangerous place to work and all. I said, "Dad, they are making good money." He said, "You come down here [General Motors] to make good money." No, I want to see what that's like, back and forth we went. This is years and years after now. We done moved from Collington Avenue to Chester Street, 924 North Chester, and naturally I'm in high school now and I've got my own little ways of wanting to do things, and my dad and I clashed, which was one of those things. I said, "Dad, I've had it. I've got to go somewhere." He said, "Son, get yourself a job."

I said, "Well, I think I've got one." At the time I am only 17, so I'm going into the service, a "minority cruise" is what they called it, but you couldn't go without your parents' consent, so my father was dead set against military, me going into the military, and my mother was--whatever I wanted to do, as moms do.

So, one weekend we are sitting up in the house in Chester Street, and I said, "Dad, I had it. We are not getting along, I just don't know what my next move is going to be. I'm asking you please sign this agreement to let me into the Navy, let me go." So, my father looked at me and he said to me, "Is that what you really want to do? Do you really want to go in the service? Is that your life, what you want to do with life?" I said, "Dad, I don't know what I want to do in life, but I know I want to go in the service now," and after that little discussion, he gives me a little pat on the back, and he said, "You are your own man. I will tell you what, when you go in that service or anything you pursue after you leave this house, you do us proud. You do us proud. You don't have to be rich, but just do us proud," and that got me off into the service.

He worked basically all daylight at GM, and in fact, after a few years he ended up being very experienced at glass cutting. They had damage on the assembly line, a big windshield or side glasses or back windows, and he would be able to take and salvage some of that. So, they created a whole unit there for him called a glass crib that he would work out of, and he would save GM and Broening Highway hundreds of thousands of dollars because he was able to take, say, a windshield and be able to cut from that windshield and make a wing window. I don't know how many out here would be familiar with the wing windows that used to be in cars, a lot of them ain't there anymore, but that's what he did, and out of his own ability to develop a piece of tool that was able to hold a glass strong enough so it wouldn't crack that he could cut that out. So, he spent the biggest part of his work life as a glass salvage person on Broening Highway, General Motors.

In fact, he also was what they call -- didn't call them Zonemen--Committeeman, that's right, he was a Committeeman and he was down there 38 years. In 1937, he worked at the shipyard and he worked four years or so, and the reason he got out of the shipyard is because he fell down a lot of holes. He lived to be able to physically live and work again, and he ended up going to General Motors because of that.

Well, when I come out after all this other little shakeup at Glenn L. Martin and finally Bethlehem Steel calls, and I get there and I'm doing my thing, that was in 1959, May 22, 1959, and in June, July of '59 is when the strike hit. So, you had to be there a certain period of time to be in the Steelworkers Union, so I was between the shit and spit, you know, because I wasn't a member yet because I didn't have my 90 days or whatever the hell it was back then to become a member. So, with that going on, that very night of the strike, I happened to be transferred from the tin mill to the hot mill on the tractor, and that was 3:00 to 11:00 shift the night of the strike. So I'm on the tractor and I am waiting for the crew to come in. The 3:00 to 11:00 crew was just leaving out of there and I'm waiting for the midnight crew to come in, and I am waiting and I'm waiting.

No crew, nobody, and I am looking and I'm looking at my watch, and I said "It's almost twelve o'clock, where the hell is everybody at?" So, I have this salary guy come out and he says, "Hey, fellow, do you want to work over?" I said, "Work over?" He says, "Yeah." I said, "Where?" He said, "Well, we need somebody to go on the picket line down there and just turn the water on do that kind of thing. When it cools down, I will let you know" – I said "Yeah, sure," not knowing any different. So, as I get off the tractor and start walking down, here comes a couple of guys up the walkway, and they said, "Hey, where are you going?" I said, "I'm going to work a double." "You will shit." I said, "What do you mean"? They said, "We are on a strike, pal. You get out of here or you are going to find your ass in that hot pit over there." It took me completely by surprise.

I have no idea who they were. I know that they wasn't kidding around when they said what they said, so I just went ahead and walked on out. I didn't even go back to the foreman who had asked to me to work over. When I walked out outside the gates, there were guys all standing around with their signs and all what have you, and I'm looking, and I thought I don't know what the hell to do. Nobody is telling me anything, I'm not in the union so they are not talking to me, so I was sort of confused. So, I walk up to one guy there, and I said "Hey, what am I supposed to do?" He says, "Who are you?" I said, "I'm an employee." "Are you in the union?" I said, "No." "Well, you ain't nothing, pal, you ain't even got a job. Get the hell out of here. Join the union," that's what he said to me, and I'm shocked, I'm totally shocked.

No one had said anything to me. No. It may have been going on, but me, I didn't pay much attention to what was being said because I'm the new guy on the block, and I'm not even in the union, that's not even involving me at this point as I took it as my understanding of it. It just seemed to me the way that those who were union were so proud of their union that unless you was a member, they wouldn't even talk to you. That's just the straw and the pride that they had, and it took a while to really see through all this, and for me. Anyway, when I finally got into the union, while they were still on strike, so they gave me a chance to get involved because I convinced one of the guys back there -- I'm trying to think, it was either Ed Plato or Al Summers, I don't know, one of those guys back there who was a union official.

I happened to go down there one day to see what's going on, what was happening to me and how do I get back to work, and I run into this guy, and [Ed]Plato I think it was, and he had said to me, "Who are you?" I said, "My name is LeRoy McClelland, Sr. I'm a tractor operator in the tin mill." He said, "Are you in the union?" I said, "No, I came in May 22nd and you guys went on strike July 1st. I didn't have my days to qualify." He said, "Well, you

Workers return to Sparrows Point after the 1959 strike.

stay here today, pal, and you are in the union." I said, "What have I got to do?" "Just stay around that barrel and hold that sign up, that's all you've got to do. When they honk, you holler strike, fair, unfair, fair, unfair," whatever, so that's what I did, and then finally we went back to work.

At this time, I was on my own. In fact, I was living on Schoolhouse Lane, right down off of Sparrows Point, North Point Road. In fact, where we were at was a bungalow. My wife and I rented a bungalow from the Webers, which used to be a Weber's Boat Marina. I had got married to a woman from our neighborhood after I got out of the Navy. When we were at the naval air station, we would come home on the weekends, and me and a buddy of mine would drive on up and we went out to, of all places Gwyn Oak Park when they had the wooden roller coaster. And I seen what is now my wife of 47 years there, and I'm talking to my buddy, I said, "Hey man, look at this. I've got to get to meet her." Says, "Well, let's go do it." So, we got our uniforms on, strutting like peacocks, look at us. I went over, and I said, "Hey, hi, hon, how are you doing?" She looked at me kind of serious like to say, "What do you want," type of thing," and then we got to meet and talk, and I took her out on a date, and the next weekend we went on a date and then we ended up getting married.

We didn't have kids until -- I was about 25 before I had any kids because just getting settled in and all, and, after I come out of the service, I bought a 1958 Chevy Impala convertible with a Continental kit. I was the cock of the walk when I am going with that to pick up my now wife. We used to drive around, go to different places and all, and then we decided to get married, and we did. She was living in an apartment on Broadway, and she had a job and what used to be Eastern Venetian Blinds, so when we start going together and then we decided we were going to get married, I had said to her, I said "Look, if we get married, you are not going to work, that's not the intent. We don't need you to work. I'm working for Sparrows Point making big money, we don't need you to work."

So she didn't hesitate to say yes or no about it, but to this very day she hasn't worked a lick, other than housekeeping. If I don't say that now and she sees this tape, I will be in deep water, but that's the way that worked. We ended up at Webers, which used to be a schoolhouse right there on Schoolhouse Lane, and the Webers -- Frank, who was a captain of the Baltimore County Police Department, Annabel, who was a retired teacher who taught at that very building--that's their home. It's also a boat yard, I don't know what it is today. I haven't been there in such a long time. Their son, Frankie, who had an eye problem, it was sort of like a roving eye, tried to get on the State Police, and they denied him because of his appearance. I don't know why I am telling you about this. But anyway, he talked to me back and forth, and I said, "Look, why don't we go to the eye clinic at John Hopkins Hospital and see whether that really has anything to do with your ability to see." So, we did, and accordingly, the roving eye was an asset because he could be looking at you and also could be watching whatever might be going on over here. But after the medical examination approved, everything was A-OK physically, he got into the State Police. I don't know what he does today in the State Police, what rank he is, but that was just one of those things you run across people that are close to you.

Shift work for me was tough because when we first got our training, it was all daylight, and once we qualified, then we were put on different schedules. It became a little bit of an adjustment, but I guess if it wouldn't be for the people you work with and the closeness, it would have been a tough change. In some shifts we would work two daylights, two three to elevens and a midnight in the same week, and then we would go on what was a 20 turn, which you would end up going Friday night into Saturday, and then that's 3:00 to 11:00, and then you would double over into the first shift Sunday morning, which would be five midnights, and then you would roll into three 3-to-11's and five daylights. It was quite a challenge to adjust. In fact, it got to a point where you didn't know whether you were going to eat or sleep or take a crap, your system was so screwed up.

Well, there's another part of explaining the steelworker and what took place down there at Sparrows Point and on North Point Road, because that's exactly what happened. In fact, you got so close that your actual home life didn't really exist as a home life should have existed. With me, with the guys and the manhood type of thing and the competition of the steel and being a steelworker, we would stop off on the road and have a few, shoot pool, darts and bullshit. We bullshit -- we rolled more steel in those bars than we actually rolled in the shift when we were working, but in that atmosphere, you didn't even think about your kids. In my point, I was lucky because the first five years we didn't have any kids, it was just her and I, but you didn't think much of her either, I mean your own wife. She made her own little life at home while you were working and you come home, sometimes you come home and be a little tipsy. So, you are trying to convince her that you are not and that doesn't work because you end up getting a cold fish, so it become a part of your life. You adapted to it.

With me as time went on and we had children and my style didn't change because at that time I really embraced the union. I embraced the purpose of the union and people like Neal Crowder, who I have immense respect for, because here I'm a young guy, and he's a guy who has actually opened the door for organized labor in Sparrows Point as far as I'm concerned. I don't know many others. Lee Douglass, I knew at times, and they all shared that purpose of making it sure that the work atmosphere was safe and healthy. That I guess is what really turned me on to being part of the organization and getting deeper into it because I realized that the company doesn't talk to the individual employee. They do talk to the representatives, and to have your voice heard, I realized that a representative was where I wanted to get into.

There were people in the mill who told us about the old days. Well, Duke was one of them. He was a roller up on the mills. I don't know his full name. In fact, that's another thing, a lot of us really didn't know our full name, and we had nicknames. In fact, we never wore steel hats, we never had the hats, never had the glasses. It was just steelworkers, and we were invincible, we couldn't get injured. That was not in our makeup that we had.

But Duke, and there was a couple other guys that were nonunion, flatly nonunion, hated the union. The reason I think -- with Duke, because I got the chance to sit and talk with him on the same shift because I was feeding the tractor for the mills and we had a breakdown and we were sitting in the cool down room because it got hot as it could be in that mill during the summer. Cold as it could be in the winter, and we would be sitting in there and he would be talking about the union and how degrading it is, and then it sort of hit me a little hard.

I said "Hey, Duke, let me ask you a question. Why do you feel so strongly against the union?" He said, "LeRoy, I had my own way. I had my way of getting things done, and if I want to work this shift, I could work this shift, and if I didn't want to roll a certain product, I didn't have to roll it, but with the union everybody has to be treated fairly, equally. I don't like that. Never liked it. I was here before the union came and I despise it for that."

I said, "Duke, I understand why you are so bitter. Let me tell you what, equality is-- something we all should be looking for. You are selfish, you are self-centered. You are a person who really needs a lot of help." That didn't get off too good because he jumped in my face, "Look, you little young punk, as far as I'm concerned, you're not ever going to be on this mill again. I'm going to see to it they schedule you somewhere else," and I just happened to look at him, eyeball to eyeball, I said, "I will tell you something, Duke, I'm a union person and the union will make sure I have my scheduled job. See you here tomorrow on the same shift," which happened, and as time went on.

There is some of that truth in that, but there is other things that took place on the shift, some sudden change or something that affected your life is what it really did. In my case, what affected me was what I had said earlier, the safety and well-being of a person working and how close -- if it hadn't been for guys like Neal [Crowder] and the union being so strong willed and their members being dealt with fairly, squarely, safely and what have you, who knows if I would even be sitting here in front of this camera by the way, because it was not a safe place to work, no matter what anybody thought. You had to take precautions, and some people become so accustomed to doing what you are doing on the job that if something was to happen out of the norm, they wouldn't be prepared to deal with, and asbestos, chemicals and stuff like that has taken its toll. As you can see, if you get an opportunity to take the picture down there in front of 2609, the monument that recognizes those who lost their lives at Sparrows Point, you would see that death wasn't a thing that didn't happen. It did happen.

Steelworkers thought they were invincible, and it affected safety and health. Yeah, I think it did, and I think when I watched some of the older guys take chances, I associated that with being a steelworker and I think that image stuck there for a long time. Did we want to wear hard hats? No. Did we want to wear safety glasses? No. Did we want to wear gloves? No. Why? Because I'm a steelworker, and that sort of was a hard image for the safety procedures to take hold, and some guys were punished or penalized for not wearing safety equipment, and I guess, being what was and what was done because of necessities of injuries and guys resented it.

I mean, there would be times probably right to this very day we would go down in the mill, there would be somebody in that mill who didn't have their safety glasses on. You would see it. It's just something that is there, or a hat, safety hat. Most cases -- in fact, by the way, now that you mentioned that hats, we resented that hat so bad we went on strike, we walked out of the mills over the hat issue, because we didn't want to be identified from what department we were working in, because we had some guys would move from one mill to the other--walk around, talk to their buddies, their father, their uncles or cousin, sister, brother or whatever. But when they brought in the hard hats, they brought in coloring of the hard hats and that identified who worked in the tin mill, who was orange; the coal mill, which was red, and then so forth, so forth, the hot mills and the rod mills and the open-hearth steel side. They were all identified differently.

But the electricians had the same color hats, and mechanics had the same color hats, so our point was why are they departmentwise in every mill with same color hat and we, because we're tin mill, have to wear orange, especially -- it was everywhere, all the production except for maintenance. Maintenance people didn't have to wear the same different color hats in different mills. They wore the same color hat and that was a little issue that irked us for that reason by the way and -- well, anyway, we lost the issue because the union, which it was right, didn't want to arbitrate an issue where the company supplied safety equipment. You are going to take that before an arbitrator who is going to look at you and say, "What are you nuts, they are looking after your safety, you can't argue that issue."

That's true we wanted to have a little free time. I will elaborate a little bit on that because there was a little bit of freedom of action there. Sometimes --you know, because we had a card system back then. It was a card, a time card you clicked in, you clicked out. Sometimes depending on how the shift was running, some guys would like to jump out of there early, go fishing or maybe grab a beer before he got home or whatever have you, the other guy would take the card and click it out back then. But even though that liberties were available, there was never ever a delay in operations because what would happen, if the unfortunate happened, the person who normally wouldn't do a certain job would do that job just to keep the operation going, but that was sort of the perks that we had.

Well, now you enter into another part of the change, and that's technology. When we looked at the safety aspect of it we knew that there were certain procedures that could protect certain things from happening, but with that protection in mind it took technology to put it in place, so that meant a job was no longer necessary. So, when you are looking for one issue to resolve another, sometimes you've got to take the outcome of it, too. And in our case with technology being advanced and computers and what have you, we've had operations that would never ever operate unless you had a person there. Now, that's not necessary. In fact, it can have a crew --it used to be six people on a mill reduced to three. Why? Computer, and then it advances further on down the road for technology. When that happened, too, you've got to understand that the idea of the union was to protect jobs, create jobs, not eliminate jobs. Well, I had the unfortunate experience of being the zone committeeman at the time when a lot of this technology was starting to really grow.

It really started in 1975, from '75 on, '80, '90s, biggest part being in the '80s really, the advanced technology. But when these other things started to take place, guys and gals sort of looked at this change coming down, felt "Hey, that's not a godsend," not realizing that when that takes place, you ain't going to be there to see it because your job is going to be gone. So, we would have meetings, I would have department meetings up here trying to make that message as clear as I could, I guess to soften the idea that "Hey, we're going to be losing jobs." That protection that used to be there is not going to be dependable anymore. You can't defend something that's no longer necessary, so we had to take these strong measures, and in my case you could find my name on every bathroom shit house wall in Sparrows Point, because I was wanting these guys to – I saw the road coming real fast at me and realized technology is going to replace jobs, and if nothing else, gain something from it. So, I was sort of accused of selling people for jobs and jobs for job classes, and all that sort of gets caught up in the big mess in itself, but it's nothing you can do. I mean, reality is that technology is the future and competitiveness is strong. If you can't deal with competitiveness, if you don't have tons per hour and manpower per hour was the way it was, and that's what had to happen.

In 1974, we negotiated an extended vacation schedule. It was supposed to encourage those finally who never had a day off, other than whatever week they were deserved, give 13 weeks, 7 weeks for those junior, but 13 weeks, and the mindset then was if they took this 13 weeks off, they would see a part of life that they missed as a worker and a shift worker and all the years they have been there and they would sort of settle into the idea that they will retire. Well, it worked somewhat, but it backfired on a lot, and then they realized that they have to eliminate the 13 weeks vacation, which they did do, and then a lot of other things started to unveil itself, like the Consent Decree, which was so misunderstood.

I never got it. No. In fact, I was just about qualified for it and they eliminated it that very year. Some of them said that they hated it, they absolutely hated the 13 weeks, and I could understand it. Christ, they spent close to 35 years of their lives in shift work in the conditions that they worked under, and suddenly they got all this free time. They wasn't adjusted for that. I mean they would get four weeks' vacation or whatever the scale. Five weeks I think was the most we could get with 20 years, 25 years or whatever it was, but 13 weeks was just a bit too much.

Well, I think the retirement part, the thing that really slowed down those thinking of retirement and the reason why there is availability of retirement is because the money was so good. I mean they were making money hand over foot. I mean, there was overtime. In fact, that was another downfall, I thought, but they didn't give much worth what I thought, was that working overtime means you are eliminating another job from being hired on, and that became such an obsession with some people that they didn't want to hear that. Hire who for what? The atmosphere started to change strongly because of the opportunity, and I kind of think that guys like myself who would say "Well, wait a minute, Christ, if you are going to work a four or five-day week, and you are going to double every day that week, that's another person that could be working here, that's another member that could eventually be a union member." And there was so much greed in that area that it didn't take off in any way. It became a part of "What are you trying to do to me, that's my living. Why do you want to screw up my living? The hell with that person over there or out there." We don't even know who he is or she is or whatever, so it was sort of that kind of atmosphere of greed.

My opinion? I think it did hurt the union. I think the membership's dwindling the way it has to this very day because they filled overtime by allowing overtime, and, in fact, now that you mention that, even out of the 13 weeks, you could sell it back. In my opinion, that was a big mistake, because that really denied others from taking advantage of what they could have gained from that. But yeah, it allowed them to sell it back, and when they said that to me, and I had said again I'm not a vibrative person, but that's the way it is, but I said "Why in the hell would you take 13 weeks that was negotiated to have a person take and allow them to sell back? That don't make any sense." And if, in fact, they would sell back a portion of their vacations, they would work in the place of overtime. I mean the whole thing became so damn ironic, it was hard to focus on what we were really trying to accomplish here.

In fact, there was never a big need for lots of money. You survived, you are comfortable, you've got necessities of life, and I think that's all we were ever looking forward to receiving. Me, again as time goes on and you gain seniority and you are looking at these benefits that the union negotiated in good faith, they really took me right where the sun don't shine, because I couldn't believe that they could do to us what they did [declare bankruptcy]. The ironic twist here is that the manager, the CEO of Bethlehem corporation, really was one who stepped out of the picture and allowed this guy Steve Miller, who came in with this big "I got a plan and the plan is we'll take this place out of bankruptcy, we won't hit bankruptcy, we won't do this."

Well, we accepted that with open arms, and we said –and I'm retired by this time--right on that coffee table you will see all my grandsons. I've got 42 years I felt under my belt. I survived. I felt good. I felt looking down the road the negotiating factor of our pension, our health coverage and everything was all done, it was set. It was in a lock box I thought, and then here in 2001, I retired. Then all hell breaks loose on December 18th, 2002. And just prior to that, we're hearing these strong rumors, which none of us would believe, you ain't telling me - even this very day you've got a hard time convincing me even though it's over, that Bethlehem Steel doesn't exist. That can't happen, it's impossible, but as we all know it has happened and it's done, it's over, but here I sat after this thing started to take off and with Miller at the head of the helm, started to get into what really was about. His forte was to take over and rape the companies of benefits of the employees, and that's exactly what this Miller did. That's exactly what he is going to do to Delphi. That's exactly what he's going to do to General Motors.

Now, I sat back here with a pension that I thought was safe in a lock box, as I said, which it isn't. My pension is coming from the PBGC [Pension Benefit Guarantee Corporation], which is a government agency, which still this very day is an estimated pension, which I have no idea of whether I'm going to owe them money. Finalize it and say, "This is your final pension, this is what you are going to receive until the Lord takes you." I have no idea whether I am going to be on the plus side or the minus side. Unique thing here is we all had a pow-wow with the PBGC, and they said right in front of us that "Look, there is a bright side, if" -- now the word is "if"—"if we have underpaid you, we will pay you a lump sum with interest." Yeah, well, don't hold your breath waiting for that lump sum with interest because that ain't going to happen.

The other side of that is that if they overpaid us, we will pay them back 20 percent without interest. Big hearts. Now mine goes since 2001, and however they figured that in between 2001 and 2002, December 18th, I have an obligation to pay PBGC since they didn't take it over until December 18th of 2002. I have never gotten a respectful answer of why I'm penalized for that period of time that had nothing to do with the bankruptcy until it was official and the PBGC jumped in--in my mind jumped ahead of creating the pensions.

I got a year's worth of benefits from Bethlehem Steel then between 2001 and 2002 until when they declared bankruptcy. Between that and I had stock, which we all had with our bargaining units, and I was advised to sell that stock because it ain't going to be worth the paper it was printed on. I said "You ain't telling me that twice." I don't like the sounds of it because that was part of the reality that was starting to focus in to where, yeah, this is really going to happen. I had guys, Christ, call my house here. That phone would ring off the hook with guys saying, "This ain't true, LeRoy, they are bullshitting us, ain't they? This ain't going to happen." I said, "Well, I wish I could sit here and tell you yeah, that's right, it's bullshit, but I can't tell you that."

It's almost like the end of the world. It is, as far as us guys go. I mean me, here I sit with three beautiful grandchildren, two of them are teenagers, the other one is five-year-old who today is with her mother and father at Disney World. In fact, not because of grandpop here, but because they were a little more frugal with their monies to be able to do that. But I look forward to doing that kind of thing. I look forward to having comfort and comfortable living here for what's left. The golden years was supposed to be that, golden years. No, golden years now is horrible. It's frightening. You sit here, I'm on Medicare. You wonder whether Medicare is going to continue to function the way we know it should, but there's going to be problems. Social Security, I've got a Social Security coming in, OK. Well, we're not sure whether Social Security is going to stay stable. There's so much of this in the area of privatizing, it's frightening as hell.

Those two areas, Medicare and Social Security are the backbone of the seniors across this country. Privatizing is going to really devastate it. Nobody can bullshit me with that because that's what's going to happen. Their vision is to have the younger workers of this very day finance their own pensions and finance their own health plans. That's their goal, and here we sit out here wondering -- as I said before--when that mail comes today, is my pension check going to be there? Is my Social Security check going to be there, or am I going to get a notice from Medicare telling me that they upgraded, which they already take $88 now out of my Social Security check for coverage of Medicare, but you have to have health, you have to have the supplement to go with Medicare because it doesn't cover the entire medical needs.

So, the golden years, just think about it. Here we sit back, we are just as -- I guess just as concerned about what we would have been if I was working week to week, paycheck to paycheck. I'm sort of working paycheck to paycheck monthly now, which is more frightening.

Yes, I do a lot of lobbying for seniors. In fact, May 10th, the timeframe is not really focused in here, but May 10th [2006] we're going to take a bus over to Washington for Medicare under the Alliance of Retired Workers. We're going under that organization to give them support.

I think what's happening to us, SOAR, Steelworkers Organization of Active Retirees, beautiful organization, people are really seeing for themselves and it's affecting them. That their fixed income is going to be disturbed. Their fixed income is a frightening figure to think, because there's no way you can have additional monies coming in because that's all you got. You can't find a job. If you are, you are silly because you just spent 42 years of your life, me particularly, and I'm looking for another job to survive? Bullshit, I live in America, I paid my dues. Now I expect to be taken care of until the man upstairs says "Hey, it's your turn."

We are seeing people who realized and are waking up and said, "Holy shit, it's me, it's not Joe Blow down the road, it's me." I'm finding more people who became couch potatoes absolutely wanting to get up and get answers, and that's healthy. When you have senior people asking questions, that's healthy. When you have senior people, who are willing to take the time of what they have left and be heard, that's healthy. So, there are a lot of things that are going on out there that are healthy and workable, but it all revolves around politicians.

I never thought about running for office. Well, in honesty I don't think I could handle that. I couldn't handle the mistrust, the misleading and the bullshit that comes out to "What you want to hear is what I will tell you." I don't think I can handle that. I think what I can handle is I get a few times that I get an article in the paper and it sort of relieves some of the stress, frustration. It's like writing in a diary. I get some things that really bug me, and I figure the only way I can get that point out is to get an article in the paper, Letters to the Editor or call my senator. In fact, it's got to a point that I'm on the Internet more than I see my wife. Some of the guys down there at the hall, they all said "Christ, if you want to get LeRoy, you better go to his house because he's on the damn computer and he ain't going to get off of it," that kind of thing.

Learning how to use a computer was a bit of a challenge because everything we did before was pencil and paper, and it was a challenge, and in fact, I didn't think I would like it, I really didn't. My wife is the one who really got started on it, and she got it basically for games and then it advanced into other things. I happened to go down the cellar here and we've got two computers down there, which I bought one for me, one for her, and I didn't want to tell her I didn't know, so I was trying to just ease my way across to get her to show me what these -- God, I can use a typewriter, always can use a typewriter, but the keys are -- they do different things and you can screw up very easy if you hit the wrong key or be something on the websites, you can really create a problem. So I got down there a couple times, just watched what she was doing. She said, "Well, do you want to learn this?" I said, "I don't want to learn nothing, just go ahead and do what you are doing," but I watched her, and one night I went down there by myself and I got on the web and I was so overwhelmed by things that I could get on the web, the web addresses, the e-mail addresses that you can get and the information. I got more information about our politicians, I got more information about what is going on in Annapolis, I got more information on what's going on in the Senate and the Congress right there firsthand. I don't have to wait for the newspaper the next day, it's right there. I can get into every newspaper in this country and get what's going on and whatever is happening in that country that very day.

It just engulfs you, and then the fear of the computer doesn't exist anymore. And even at work, when the transition of computerization took place, we used to take our scrap buckets, big buckets, big bins I should say, and haul them down there and weigh them. We used to have a scale man there. To show you how advanced that got with technology, they eliminated the scale person and they put a scale there, and all you had to do was hit certain buttons, boom, boom, boom, and it would weigh it, it would give you a card in return of what the weight was and you put the box there and the scrap crane come down and dumped it. You put it back to your place and turned in the weight, and it was all computerized, and they simplified it because they had a red key -- a monkey could have done it. That's what they were dealing with, the transition, and with technology. Also, a lot of guys did leave the mill because they were embarrassed, they couldn't make the mental change from using the keyboard to using the hands on.

Yes, technology absolutely did drive them out. And change is tough for anybody. With me, I'm lucky to be able to experience what I did from -- example, from the Navy from reciprocating engines to jet engines. You went into these different phases, but it didn't scare you because it was a challenge.

It was like moving from Collington Street to Chester Street. It wasn't easy for me to decide to do that with the comforts of home, but Dad and I just didn't hit it. We kept on getting into different areas, and I knew he was doing it for the good reasons, he was doing it to make a man out of me. That's what he was doing it for, not to run away from something, just to do that, but then I have my own mindset, I'm a teenager, I'm hot to trot. "Dad, you live your life, you want me to live my life, sign the papers."

Yeah, here at home, all my kids were born and raised here, 451 Corner Road, right here. I moved here in 1962 I think, '60, '62, somewhere in there. I had been at Sparrows Point about three years. And now, from here on the beltway, I could get there in fifteen minutes depending on whatever backup they might have.

Oh, yeah, the shift work did affect me here. Did the union affect me here? If it wouldn't be for my wife, the kids didn't raise themselves, she raised them, because I would be either at work or I would be at the union function. I would be out of town, I would be at Linden Hall, I would be in Pittsburgh or I would be over in Washington. Again, we were married 47 years and it takes an immaculate woman to do what my wife has done all this time. Even though we argue, don't get me wrong, it's not a perfect marriage. We argue, we have our difference of opinions, but that's what I love about her, she has her own opinion. I can't influence her. I can tell her certain things, and then if she doesn't agree, that ain't going to happen. If it ain't going to happen, it ain't going to happen.

But anyway, with the kids, all of them were educated here. They went to the elementary school here, Middlesex Elementary. They went to Kenwood. Stemmers Run, then Kenwood [High School] and they could walk. It's a really old-fashioned existence. Yeah, and in fact right now -- this is a row home, I don't care what anybody says. "Townhouse" is what they call them, but it's a rowhome, but the community it's changed, it's changed quite a bit now since then, since when they were brought on this earth. The closeness that was there and friendship and kids, you didn't have to worry about them, didn't worry about some guy stalking your kids, you didn't worry about dope, you didn't worry about any of that until they got older. Then you worried about it because that seemed to be what you always see on the news or in the paper, these kids on dope, this one is taking cocaine and this one, you know.

Yeah. I think the biggest part of it, yes, the basis -- you and I may not be on this earth, but the generation that does exist--jobs itself, availability, is not going to be here because everything we have done in this country has been an outsourcing and we are outsourcing every day of the week. I mean we're talking about -- here, my daughter who worked 12 years at Hecht's, it's no longer a Hecht's, they bought her out. They give her a buyout, or she can go to Macy's, but I think it's Macy they are now, she can go there but not where she was originally working at in Whitemarsh. She would be somewhere where they needed her. She is raising a five-year-old. She just can't jump and go. So that change is brought on. Places like Wal-Mart, Sam's, Dollar Stores, I mean, people don't realize this is why the economy in this country is going down the tubes because we are not exporting anything, we are importing. We are importing more, and when you import, the jobs necessary to make the product isn't needed here because it's done outside.

Our own steel industry, our steel industry, Mittal, now here is a global giant of steel. He has got operations all around the world. Before it's over with, this person, this family is going to end up absolutely controlling the price of steel, and here America sits, when defending this country is going to depend on getting steel from other sorts of the world or other parts of the world. What a challenge that's going to be. Right now, Mittal has shut down operations here. Why? Because he has places around the world. Weirton Steel, they shut down the steel side completely. No way down the road are they going to open, reactivate it. It is over. So that's one section. And when that character came here, he made it clear that if productivity becomes a problem, then that place is gone, and he ain't just saying that to threaten them. He said it and meant it, and it's happening.

What I see going to come down here again, and this is just me-- this is me, my wave length, my tunnel, sometimes tunnel vision, but it turns out that Weirton Steel produces a better tin plate than Sparrows Point. I say -- and my son who works there right now, he's an operator on the halogen lines--I said, "John, don't be surprised if some of your operations here starts shutting down permanently. Do not be surprised." Lo and behold, there's no more chrome line down there. Where is it? Weirton. Well, it's just a matter of time before some of the other operations that used to depend on the tin mill to supply them will not be operating there.

Well, you know, the ironic twist here, is Weirton is an independent union. So, the affiliation between our union and theirs seems to already have a stumbling block. Now, that probably -- will it ever be done? I don't know, I don't know how to answer that. I don't think so. I think the independency of that union is so strong that the will of theirs is going to control whatever may happen.

What I did say, and caught heat over this, I did say when them guys went out on strike, that our union should go down and show support and strength. I did say that. I caught hell over that. "They are nonunion." Well, they are an independent union. They are not a nonunion. They are an independent union, there are two different worlds there. You've got to merge those worlds. United Steel Workers of America took the step to make sure the merging and strength of this North America organization is now known as the United Steelworkers. Not America, United Steelworkers. Why? Numbers. That's why. Well, why should we give up – and I'm a hard liner on this--why should I give up what I was raised in, what I basically built my whole union attitude around was the United Steelworkers of America? I'm not going to change that for any reason. I will go to my death with that. In fact, my license plate out there is 30-USWA, United States Steelworkers of America. So, I understand compromise, don't get me wrong. I don't want to be confusing here. They do these things to survive, but what they better do, they better go back more strongly towards their retirees.

I think the focus of some of the organizations that are starting to crop up, like reunions, is to bring back the strength of what retirees have. If organized labor doesn't really look stronger at their retirees--I'm talking about our group, we are known as 2609 and 2610, which now is 9477. Our identity is still 2609. Now, I'm not opposed to seeing 2609 and 2610 merge together. I am opposed for them to change their locals. I'm opposed to that. Does that mean anything? I doubt it.

There was a point in having two locals because of the 30,000 people, but as they lost membership, the merger would have probably been more sensible at the time. But then you've got to enter the other little square called "politics." That's meaning one local politician group, president all the way down to the executive board, then the other local -- somebody has to give up power, and that was not an easy transition to take place or it wasn't an agreeable type thing that had to be decided and was decided, and that's where you ended up with 9477.

With us, again I'm trying to emphasize the fact that the foundation of all unions reflects the retirees. They are outspoken, they have experienced it and they walked the walk and they talked the talk, but they are not showing the respect for us that they should. Our international union has done a great thing in a prescription program. They did a great thing there, there's no question about it, but they could do more. They could do much more for the retirees. They have in my mind this hunger to increase membership, but it's like shuttling shit against the tide, it ain't going anywhere because we are outsourcing. So, if organized labor doesn't take and absolutely merge all international unions into one strength, then God help us.

Today, I will give you a good example of the Latinos. You will see a good example of that because today is to show even the illegal immigrants in this country are part of this, that show the strength that they are going to provide, which is manpower, and no telling what that's going to lead to.

I think people my age have a much greater appreciation for the union. Well, yeah, I absolutely do that, too, and I will tell you why. With my own son, he's a young guy and he doesn't see -- at this point now, I'm not saying it's because of me. "Dad, I don't see the need for it any more," and that's falls fault in the fact that we entered into this partnership thing that really blowed up in our face. It wasn't actually a partnership. It was just to see how much more they could control, and if we ever lose the union and lose the organizations, then you are talking about a right to work state, that's what you are talking about, so everybody will be individualized. They will all be "me, me, me," and "I, I, I," and there will be no "you and us," and that's frightening in itself.

We sometimes have hot discussions. I mean they were all born under the house with a union and they always will be when they step in that door-- it's union, and we sit down, and we have a quiet type of political type of conversation. My son's latest was they had a reelection down there, and he was asking my opinion about certain people, and he sees the need to, or he did see the need, that his old crew were balking at the idea they want to eliminate another job, so they want to sort of slow the work down. My son said "Dad, I'm down there to make money. If the line doesn't run and I don't make a profit, then what's the sense of me being there?" And the conversation went into this direction. I said, "Well, John, I understand your plate, I understand what we are all looking at down the road, but let me tell you what a crew is, what it means. A crew works together, it's teamwork. If you can't work with your crew, you are going to become all alone, you're going to be out on that island by yourself, so if you want to live that way, that's your choice, you are a man, make that choice." Well, what do you think? I think "Well, John, I think you ought to do what that team wants to do and become that team player with the union. I'm not talking company. I'm talking union, I'm talking about your own crew. If you lose credibility with your crew, then you are going to lose all respect that you have gained. So, my suggestion to you is go with the crew, not go with the flow, go with the crew," and he did, I learned later.

I learned about the union from Neal Crowder. Neal worked the CA line. He was an operator on the CA line—Continuous Annealing. Well, what it does is heats the metal. It's a coil form and it heats the metal so it can be skin milled on the skin mills. It's a process, a metallurgical process is what it does.

Neal, by the way, because I was on the tractor that was feeding the coils to the CA line, and Neal would be on the other end, the operator would be --well, he would be on the middle, and a couple of nights, I would walk down and because we have a breakdown waiting for the electrician or the mechanics, we would talk, and he would talk about the strength and the unity and all that was necessary. Remember, I'm just coming out of the Navy and experienced half of what I have seen here. I'm still overwhelmed by the hugeness of the operation. It's just a whole new world when you walk into that mill, the things that go on around you.

It just took a lot to adjust to the idea that all that exists. So Neal and I would talk, and he would tell me about the need of being together and all, and I had spoken to him about the issue that was starting to really surface--the black and white issue, and then Neal had said a few things that he felt that they wanted and how it should never have been that way. But at that time, that's the way things were, and the thing that --well, what he was more focused on was to assure management that they wasn't going to dominate the employee. Then the union took its hold and did what it had to do and gain recognition, which grew out of people – if it had not been for people like Neal, who was in the mills, not out there on the gates handing out literature. He was in that mill, took jeopardizing his job, by the way, when he went out to solicit and promote the idea of being a union member. We talked about other things and then he really got me interested in being part of the union, like Marianne Wilson--she was another one who was a very strong person and for people's rights and female's needs and the whole nine yards with that.

That atmosphere between the two of them, plus others like Dave Wilson and Harry Spedden and Kellner--which I've got a story I can talk about with him and I through the years that differ, different things--and so many guys. Steve Hamilton was a tractor steward, black guy tractor steward. Steve Griffith was a tractor steward. Robin -- there's so many guys and gals that you cross as you got older and seniority went across their trails, but my real desire was to see change. My real desire was, first off, to become president of that local union somewhere down the road, which never happened. I failed it. I tried. I stepped out of what we call the BJ zone, which was a caucus, which I was at one of time the chairman of. Got that political bug about "I want to have a stronger voice, I want to be able to make my point and be heard," and I felt the position of president would do that. So anyway, as we move along with this, guys like Kellner influenced me getting involved.

Well, committees. I started off with a committee. I was asked to be a blood bank committee person, and I said "Sure, I've got no problem with that." So as time went on I become the blood bank chairman, and then I become a trustee of Local 2609, and then that give me a good feel for the inside politics of what organized labor really leads into. They are different than the politician on the corner, because you want to do things that make you identifiable so when your time comes for reelection people remember who you were, compared to who is challenging you, that kind of thing.

Dave Wilson was the president back then. Primo Padeletti was the District Director, that's who it was, and then Wilson challenged him down the road. The locals were very big and contentious. In fact, our two locals, 2610 and 2609, were so strong in their beliefs separately, it got to a point where the parking lot down there, they put a chain up there. It's attitude, it's all about attitude, and then things started to mellow out and then the chain came down and some of the other things that were unmentionable were resolved, but all through this, all through this gaining this experience and you are actually walking the walk, you are right there seeing things being decided on, the directions to be sort of measured out, what have you.

I will never forget the strike. We came back to prevent a strike. We were all in Pittsburgh, John Cirri, me, Kellner, and there was one other guy. Frank Rossi, I think it was. This is 1985, '85 or '86. We avoided a strike, and the reason it was so important to avoid it because our own language in the contract prevented it. And this was at a time, a very tough time in the steel industry, concession bargaining. Lloyd McBride had a heart attack over it.

It got such good coverage on this ourselves, because all this was all happening. The answers that would be easily gotten weren't, so your reactions was immediate, you done what you needed to do and do it now, and I questioned it. Just do it. But we were all up there in negotiations when this took place, while this was going on. So, we all jump in my car and I'm beating all back Route 70, coming down 70 through Breezewood, yeah. We used to stop in a Breezewood restaurant there. We would buzz on down. Anyway, I got stopped by a State Police. In fact, we are going down there, one cop is under the bridge, he's got a camera going on. Somebody in the back seat said, "LeRoy, there's a cop." I said, "Piss on that cop, we've got to get going," and I'm looking in the rearview mirror, I don't see him. While I'm looking in the rearview mirror, half a mile down the road here's a guy that walks right out in the middle of the highway, and I think it was John Cirri, "Christ, there's a cop." "Where? There ain't nobody there."

Boom, both feet on the brakes like this, I'm fishtailing, and holy shit. So, he pulls me over to the side, and he comes up to me, he said, "Where are you going, pal? What's the fire?" I said, "Hey, we've got a strike. We've got to get back to Baltimore. We've got to go now." "You ain't going anywhere," blah, blah, blah, and I says -- in fact, I don't know her husband, her husband was the lieutenant or captain of the State Police. Christ, I can't think of her name. She used to be president of 9116. Her husband was a State Police lieutenant or captain, and then I'm throwing his name out there, and the guy says to me, "Hey, let me tell you something first off. The person you are naming, this ain't his district," and I'm thinking to myself "of all the luck, ain't even his damn district," and he warned us, too, because he was there with his wife, warned us about coming back that way. So anyway, I get a ticket and we get in here.

The strike had to do with job eliminations, that is what it had to do with, and then we all gave back -- it was quite a confusing time because couldn't get any definite answers of what our next direction because we agreed not to strike. This was all internal, this was done internally. So we managed to be able to control that, and we convinced the company not to lock the gates, don't create the lockout.

People were in the street. North Point Road had them closed going into the gate going into that direction. This was not the 2609 Committee, no, these were the people, the members themselves, and we had to go down there and identify us to them because they wasn't convinced that the guys that were talking to them weren't company, just to convince them. We had to go down there and convince them "Look, this is not the route to take, blah, blah, blah, blah." So, it ended up working itself out to where no one was penalized. The company did throw in our face about the cost of operations and all that, which is normal. I said "Well, the point is that there may be a loss of tonnage, but you've got the operation back, so if you want to stir some shit up again and get some reaction like we got here that we ain't going to control, then you take that chance."

Well, you know it's ironic, some of these things that do take place with strikes and who better knows than the person on that floor who is doing the work knows what's happening? Then when things seem to not quite go its way or agree to, you've got to react. If you don't react, then there's no reaction and then you are just going to roll over and play dead, and you can't do that.

Today, though, things have truly changed, they have truly turned around. This ain't going to go off too well with others who are going to hear this tape, but my opinion with the union seemed to be rolling over a bit. Instead of taking a strong stand, they realized that it's like the waterfall, it's going to continue to come over the fall because you ain't going to be able to get over the waterfall. Outsourcing is the damnation of organized labor in this country and it better wake up and see it.

The AFL-CIO with the split that took place there, that was the worst thing that could ever happen. It's just like the controllers, the air controller strike, worst thing that could ever happen because the AFL-CIO would not support those who were not affiliated under the same umbrella of the AFL-CIO. That hurt more than it helped. Strength of the organized labor is numbers, numbers make it count. People support the movement for what it's there for, and what is it there for? It's there for guys like me who retired looking forward to where they spent their life, knowing that they are going to have at least a comfortable rest of their lives to live out, what there may be. I sit in front of this camera right now with asbestos. It's scary. It's a slow degrading disease that eventually will take its toll. When? Can't tell that. It could be tomorrow. Do I have sufficient signs? Like you don't see no oxygen bottle yet. That's not here. Is it going to be there? If I live long enough to need it, yeah, it will be there. That's like a lot of us, and I'm sort of jumping around here, but to go back with the older guys I see every third Wednesday of the month [at the retirees meeting] who were there before any precautionary things were installed and they are still here.

That just boggles my mind. The raw chemicals and the asbestos was much more raw and more fluent in the air, but they are here and they are in their 80's, and their mindset, their mind is still together, it ain't all marbles in there yet, but there will be down the road. We all face that-- Alzheimer's, dementia, all that other shit that comes with it.

Once in the union, my desire was to become the shop steward, tractor steward representative, which there were those that didn't like my attitude for some reason. I don't know why I was labeled a redneck, but I'm not a redneck. And for a lot of things that I got into, there was resentment—"Don't let him on the committee, don't let him do this." I found my way, so I went ahead and did what I did and confronted management on issues and I confronted my own brothers and sisters on issues they didn't like to hear, but that was the reality of it. Ain't no sense bullshitting it. This is the way it is and this is what you are faced with. You missed time, you face the penalty. Is that good? Is that bad? "You are my union, I pay you to protect me." No, if you don't do your old job, then you are going to find your own route. Here's the rules. You live by the rules. If they violate your rules, we burn them. You violate their rules and they will burn you. That's as simple as the philosophy was.

Then I moved on up into the secretary of the grievance committee after I become the BJ zone committeeman, which in that day was a powerful position to hold, so much so that Kellner and I used to go head to head because he used to be -- not used to be, he always was very protective of the 449. That was his group, backup gang. He was a millwright, and his millwright skills was to deal with big huge backup rolls, and they had collars on them. It's hard to explain it without showing a picture of it, but they were big rolls and they had to pull the collars off of them, and that's what these millwrights do.

And the big rolls pressed the steel. You have a big set of rolls and then you have the small rolls. The big set presses from the lower part and then the upper rolls press from the top, and you set the different gauges, like an old-time washing machine, so people can visualize what it looked like. Yeah, and if ever an opportunity -- there are many movies out there, you can see operations of that. It's just you take -- they can roll steel as thin as the hair on your head or as thick as the beams you see out here. So, I mean the operation is something else, but Kellner and I, he had been his own committeeman before, and he stepped up to recording secretary and then stepped up to president. Well, there was a lot of other little movements that went on, and a guy by the name of Ray Pazinski who was the Zoneman before me. He was an operator on the prep lines.

Now I was satisfied with being the tractor steward, representing the tractor department, I was satisfied with that, gained experience and meeting people and situations. You sort of adjust to the needs that you have to put a focus on, the things that interest you most and what concerns the member--what they expect to see or hear from you and what you can do and what you can't do. How the company respects you for one thing, as well as your own members. That was critical and important.

So Pazinski, one night, I'm working 3:00 to 11:00, I'm putting coils on the prep line, number five prep line by the way, and I backed the tractor up. I'm sitting over there under a heater, big ass heater, not putting any heat out, but it's there. So, you are sitting there waiting for the coil to come through the units and you pick it up, take it to its destination, wherever it had to go. Pazinski says to one of the feeders, his feeder -- there was a scaleman, feeder and the operator, besides the baler operator who was down on the floor there with the baler taking the edges of the stuff that they were slitting and rolling into a bale.

He said to one of them guys, "Tell LeRoy over there that he couldn't win dog catcher," and the guy says, "I don't think you should say that." I had no idea for a zoneman, I really didn't, and the guy came over there, I'm sitting there reading the new contract with the old one, and I'm looking at him, he says, "Hey, LeRoy."

I said, "What?"

"Do you know what Ray said?"

I said, "I don't care what Ray says."

He said, "You couldn't beat him in a dog catcher race."

"He didn't say that."

"Yeah, he did. That's bullshit. I'm telling you," so he walked away, done his thing and come out and got some water.

I got off the tractor and I walked up to him, I said, "Ray, you are the zoneman now. You've been the zoneman for the last almost three years now with the election coming up. Why do you want to make a stupid comment like that? What's your problem with me?"

He said, "I'm just telling you, pal, you can't beat me in your best day."

I said, "I don't even give a shit about the zone committee job, I don't care. It doesn't bother me, but you know what, you just bothered me now and I'm going to take that job and I'm going to win that job." And then this is weeks and weeks before 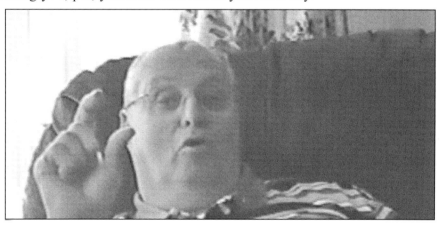 nomination. So, I belonged to the BJ caucus, which at that time Kellner was chairman of the caucus. And BJ doesn't stand for anything. That's what they did during the war. Each one of the operations down there had designated alphabetical letters. They didn't mean anything. I can add something here, but I won't, that BJ was accused of being, especially me, and I don't think it would be respectable, I don't think. I can give you a smaller version of it, "Big Joint," and then it gets a little more explicit. So anyway, as time goes on and I'm getting on walking around to different departments and getting the support of my own caucus for the zone job, which we have -- that's another unique position of organized labor within its own local units, the politics internally. You have different zones. In our case we had the different zones, the BP, the BH, the BJ, and there was one other -- well, BR was another one, and each one of those had Zonemen, and the Zonemen had Assistant Zonemen, and then they had shop stewards. It was a real structure, and within the local structure, they had committee jobs that each zone had a representative on, whatever committee that was going on, like the blood bank committee and trustees and stuff like that. Contracting out. Civil rights was a big one. Women of Steel. There were so much internal things that were going on, and just like any politics, any politics, you've got to watch what you say and who you say it to, because if that person just took a dislike to you, they would pass that word around about something you said and you would never have an opportunity to defend it to the person that they are going to repeat it to.

The campaign was a real donnybrook type of campaign, mud slide, mudslinging and finger pointing and all that kind of stuff. The biggest thing that used to come out of Ray's group was "that damn redneck from Baltimore," meaning me. And he was from here, from Highlandtown by the way, and he was a good pool shooter. So, like I say a lot of times, the camaraderie, I think, grew stronger and stronger when we would stop off after our shift at the local bars down there, and we would be shooting pool or playing darts or just rolling steel, like I said before, and Pazinski would be in there. Nine ball used to be our game. Three fingers Joe, I don't know whether that rings a bell with anybody, but he was one of the pool players in the state championships years ago and he would hustle down on North Point Road in Dundalk sometimes, too.

Anyway, we got to playing this nine-ball game and Ray was in there and he is a good shooter, good shot, he would make shots you wouldn't believe. Here I've got three sheets to the wind and he's on the table and he comes up to me and hits me on the shoulder and he says, "LeRoy, I will tell you what I will do. Play a nine-ball game, ten dollars on the nine and five dollars on the five. If you win, the election ain't an issue with me because I won." I said, "Well, that's good of you, brother Ray. Glad to hear that. Now let's get back to the nine ball. I'm not a good shooter as you are," but nine ball sometimes becomes a lucky game, things that you think you are going to do don't happen.

"Well, I ain't asking. Do you want to play or not?"

I said, "Well, I will tell you what, Ray." Barmaid comes up and I said, "Come here, hon. I want you to do something for me please. Here's $15. Ray, give me your $15 on the table, on that bar." So we go down there --this is when $15 was worth something, Christ, yes--and he flips his quarter, I get the break. I break the nine ball. I get up, I get the break, I hit the ball, the nine ball goes right in the corner pocket, ten bucks, bang. I take a couple more shots, choke up on a few shots because it looked so easy and I choked up, I was excited. Ray gets up there and bing, bing, bing, bang. Now comes the five ball. And he looks at me and he says, "Tell you what. $20 on the five ball and I will bank it side pocket." Shooting two balls from the bottom to the top and he's going to make the five ball.

I looked at him, I said, "I will tell you what, Ray. I will take that bet, but before I take that bet, bring your 20 bucks here and put it on top here and I will put mine," which I didn't have at the time. So, he put his $20 there. He didn't look for me to put mine there, right. I just folded it like that. Gets there, takes a little bit of this and chalk and all this other bullshit. He hits it, he missed. I said, "I will tell you what. I will take the five ball because now it's in the middle of the table and I will bank it on the right corner, lower right corner for five more dollars."

He says to me, "How about payday?" I said, "You're on." I didn't have my 20, remember that, so I went boom, hit it, went in. It went and fell in. He thought his whole world caved on him because all the guys around the bar said, "Yeah, he took the king down, he took the king down."

Anyway, I don't know why I even got on to that, but between the political end of this thing and the desire of people who wanted to represent the union and have a voice in the union, this kind of thing is what really created the stress, you know, besides the basic part of Neal and Marianne. Ed Bartee was another instrumental person. He used to work on the halogen lines way before my son even got a job down there. Ed Gorman, I mean these guys are all retired. Eddie Bartee is still very active.

Chris Loucas, I remember Chris Loucas. I.W. Abel, I remember some of those guys, yeah, but closer to home there was a couple -- well, like I say, it's a fact that they are right up front and sometimes they are not--that were instrumental. Len Shindell, he was a little confusing at first because some of his points of view was more like a communist point of view than it was of a solidarity group point of view, but as time went on, I think Lenny was misunderstood by a lot of people. His attitude towards things were not influenced too much by what was going on here. It was actually what was going on down at the end of the road here with him and he would give you that--that's the way it is. Do you want to hear the way it is, or you don't want to hear it? He will tell you like it is. He ain't going to soft shoe it. He always impressed me with that. He was the Zoneman for the coal mill. Jim Romano was the Zoneman for the hot mill. Larry Farinetti was the Zoneman for the VH, and I'm the Zoneman for the BJ, and George Lacy was the Zoneman for the BP, which was the pipe mill at that time.

We all would be up there for a grievance meeting at the hall. I'm the secretary of the grievance committee and Romano was the chairman of the grievance committee. We would bring up issues and complaints and resolving this or doing that. Well, with the grievance procedure, each employee -- each member I should say--would have a complaint, a grievance about an issue, either it be overtime or it would be unsafe condition or some kind of a penalty that was not properly presented. And sometimes we would get into issues as sensitive as alcoholism and drug abuse and on these grievances, we would go through the procedure--the shop steward on turn, first off that's where it begins. They complain to the shop steward, and the shop steward proceeds to see whether it's a legitimate complaint, and then if he thinks so, he will file a grievance and then it will come into what is known as step two is what we deal with in step two with management.

So before we meet with management, we would all take these grievances together the day before and we would talk about them and what has merit, what we don't think has merit, what you are going to present, what I'm going to present. We would have an agenda for the next day because that's how you had to operate here, you just couldn't bring in some spontaneous thing. It had to be on the agenda. We would meet with the company on step two, and then step three -- I'm jumped too fast. Step two is where we meet with superintendents individually, each zoneman would take their concerns to their respective superintendents, and if they didn't come out with a resolution of it, they would then push it to step three, which was the management representatives and the union representatives discussing the issues. And if, in fact, we couldn't get this resolved at that step three level, then we would arbitrate issues. Then it would go to Pittsburgh, to the staff, which would be our representatives.

In this case, in the subdistrict office would be Bill Nugent, who did a terrific job in all the years of all this transition taking place. It was a unique situation where Dave Wilson was sort of somewhat from the old school coming into the changeover school with technology and all these other things that had to be dealt with. Dave ended up being the District Director and retiring from that after a few years; in fact, I think two terms as a director. But all this time that's gone by, the changes in the mill started to really show up. You could see what this really meant with the technology and the job eliminations, which become an ugly word, but job eliminations were necessary for technology.

Yeah, I think that Bill Nugent didn't get elected [District Director] because of these changes. I think there was a lot of locals within the district that were disappointed for things that couldn't be dealt with. There was no change. I was saying to you earlier we had technology that was taking over the jobs, there was no defense. You couldn't argue an issue in front of an arbitrator if technology is put in the place because of a safety precaution, and basically that's what ended up. We used to have two people on the bailer under the prep lines on the shear floor. They would take care of the scrap and make sure that the scrap was staying lined up and all. Well, they eliminated one.

We argued that issue, we took it before an arbitrator because it's unsafe to have that person down in the hole by himself. Well, the company argued the issue of the fact that they had a camera that the operator could watch, but our argument was the operator has got all this other responsibility when the unit is running to be able to flick his eyes over here and see what's going on while the scrap is being baled up. He is watching the unit, he is watching the shearing of it, the slitting of it. In our opinions, it was just impossible for this person to be so flexible, looking all over the place, down at the teleprompter here to watch who is down in the hole and watch the sheet and watch the feeder on the other side, it's too demanding.

Well, after the arbitrator heard the issues and took the issues. A week or two later, maybe couple weeks later, his decision was in favor of the company. So there again issues -- that may have been disappointing, but that was a guideline. Guys in my mindset saw that being the issue and thought to myself "Well, if they take these other measures of safety precaution and they fall on that term 'safety precaution' and that eliminates a job, I don't have much of a defense to argue that." Just like the hat issue, you couldn't argue that. You couldn't argue the safety glasses. You didn't wear them before. Well, you didn't before, but now it's a safety issue and the company is protecting its employees. You can't argue that. So, all these things are learning steps in dealing with issues, and you wouldn't get that out of a book.

Well, I found criticism from those kinds of guys who never came to a meeting, yeah, sure. In the locker room, I would be in the locker room, they would bad mouth this issue or that issue, and my only response to that was "Hey, if you wanted to say what you are saying to me, why don't you come up the hall and say it to everybody up there so we all understand where your disgust is? But my disgust is you don't even have the decency to come to the meeting to understand what the whole issue is. You are just getting bits and parts."

By the way, that kind of an issue is dealt with every day. It depends on the guy's attitude or the girl's attitude or this one here is being treated better than me. Some of these are petty things, but they are things that they need attention on. If you ignore it and just take it as an attitude that "Hey, that's immaterial." It isn't immaterial. It's material to them and you've got to deal with it, and I felt if I tell them just like I felt, and I tell them this is where you are, then that resolves the issue. Either makes me the bad guy or at least I'm understood. That's the only point that I ever try to drive, and my personality -- I don't have what you would call a soft personality because my dad didn't bring me up that way.

And a soft personality could absolutely not survive as a Zoneman. You know why? He would be kidding himself, because you know what your limitations are. You better know. If you are going to make decisions that affect job eliminations and the repercussions that that takes --you would not believe when I tell you some of the things that I agreed to, and even my own representatives were against me to do that, and the reason they were is because politically it wasn't favorable or the safer thing to do. "Hey, that LeRoy, that redneck LeRoy over there, he is giving jobs away"-- I can't take that stand, and my only defense when I would get up and give my zone report, I would make it that this is open eyed, clear as it could be said, what repercussions will happen, when it will happen and why.

Did it get accepted? No, of course not. I joined the union to be protected and blah, blah, blah, and then if -- the thing I learned by the way, is why argue first off on the mill floor, on the union floor with a person who is already angry about an issue he don't totally understand or she don't totally understand. I don't give them that courtesy to do that, because all that does is to enrage others who are sitting there quiet, and then suddenly they become ignited, and then they all get in there, and then, before you know it you've got a donnybrook going on.

As a union rep, even as a Director or even the President of international unions, the wider scope is much more challenging, and the only army, and I use the term "army" that a union has is its members. If you don't have the numbers, then you are not going to win the argument, and then the argument you've got to make sure it makes sense. I mean why argue against an issue that's going to protect human life, because you get another aspect, some other group that comes in there that your sensitivity, you are too politically oriented, or you are doing it for you and not for them. It's all complicated.

Is there an easy solution? I don't see an easy solution. I don't think any one of us can sit down any time without a difference of opinion. If that difference of opinion never happens, then God help us there, too. We need differences of opinion, we need to be able to bounce off other ideas and see whether they are feasible and whether they are not, and it all rolls into what are we here for, what is the union here for? The union's prime function is to protect the jobs.

We also had the Partnership Agreement. Roughly, I would think it would be in the latter part of the '70s, close to '80s. Anyway, the International sent a representative down and they were telling us about some of the things that were going to come about, about partnering and teamwork and all that other things. We have been exposed to so many of these campaigns that the company put on. We had one that we really made in bad taste, left a bad taste in our mouths was "Where is Joe." That's a campaign was similar to what they were trying to, I guess. reenergize with this partnership.

The campaign was job efficiency--do more than the job calls for and that kind of thing. Well, I could sense it back then that what they are leading into was that you are not just a tractor operator, you are not just a prep line operator, you are also whatever is needed to be done in the area type of person. That's what they were really driving to get out of that, and that was eventually leading into job elimination. Now, the way they did it from the beginning was sort of slowly. Then, I guess, the real plus in management side was they went into the mill and they got to talking to the guys and the gals on the mill floor, which made them feel ten-foot-tall because management is talking to them. Here's the plant manager, here's the superintendent, so this is exposure that they never had in the past, so that was sort of winning them over to use the term like that, was winning the guys and gals over.

"What you call it talked to me." When I confronted that, I said to a couple of people, I said "Well, he talked to you, you talked to them. Didn't you talk to them? Just because they talked to you, you feel ten feet tall?" That don't make sense to me. They come to talk to you because you have something they need and what you have that they need is performance. The more performance that you do and more profit and production that goes out, that's why you are knowing their name now. Because they know your element of what you do, how important it is for you to be that gainful, productive, profit person to make profit for the company, which by the way is not a bad thought because if the company fails, we fail. So, it's hand in hand, but don't be confused about the partnership of it because that has a way of sort of absorbing you totally into the management philosophy, which is profit versus safety, so you sort of have to weigh that as it went on.

With creating quality circle teams, which was another big strong effort on management's part, that was an effort in my mind to take away the control of the zone committeemen and the shop stewards. That was to have the individuals, who by the way put me in mind of Duke who I was telling you before was definitely against the union, was a nonunion employee, and it brought me back to thinking about the way Duke thought individually, me, me, me type of thing instead of how a team is supposed to work with each and everybody together, supporting everybody's purpose in looking after everybody.

But the partnership end of it got into just what it was designed to do. It ended up in the job eliminations. It made some people feel that they are doing more with less people, and that was a frightening feeling for me to see because they were not arguing the fact that they are going to not only sit there and -- not sit there, I shouldn't use that term, but stand there watching their operations while the mill is running. You've got some idle time, take the broom and sweep over there and sweep over here, and they did this without any resistance. That was scary to me because the laborer who was on turn wouldn't be needed, and I would try to get that point across. Sometimes the resentment was "LeRoy, look, I know the superintendent, I know him and he knows me and this is the way I work." It was sort of, I guess, an overwhelming experience for some of the people to get to meet upper management, and it turned out to be a little more frightening to me to see the outcome of it. The outcome was what we see today is job elimination, and so that became technology, and then before you know it, here we are -- right now I think it's something like 2,500 people there including management. I think that's what's down there now out of 33,000 that was there at one time.

One problem with the Partnership was that you had union members disciplining other union members. Well, see, that's the only part -- I guess I missed that. When the team playing thing started to evolve, it did create that. It created a finger pointing thing of this guy or this gal, they ain't doing this really the way it should be or they are taking off. It turned out to be a type of telling on you. If you would walk off the job and sneak a discussion with somebody you fished with the day before, that person would automatically tell the superintendent. It was a tell-all type of thing it started to create, and it didn't go off, by the way. I'm sure you're aware of it by now that the partnership did go because they lied to start with. Management didn't do the partnership in which it was designed it would be done in. Each had a different method for what they wanted to do and that was to divide the union itself and its representatives in this -- I guess, its influence. So, I think the old saying is that "if you can't beat them, join them." So, management found these programs to be a joinable type of thing to win over what some people felt was -- I still feel that its own purpose wasn't to gain anything out of it other than to take control of their own employees away from the union's philosophy of job protection.

It is an ongoing battle between management and the union for the hearts and minds of the members. Yeah, and when you say something like that, you are also saying something in the direction of -- it's always kind of a battle between employee and management. Now the company is not going to profit if they don't have harmony, and harmony ain't going to be gotten to when management lies to the employees, and that seems to be their forte. They lie, they don't mean what they say.

An example of that is just why I am sitting here right now--that benefits that were, in good faith, negotiated were not lived up to. They knew and they had to know that Bethlehem was headed for bankruptcy, years before it really went to bankruptcy, but who better than Bethlehem had all the income of monies flowing and cash going out? They had them. They also knew by the way the lifespan of their operations, their machinery. They knew they were coming to closely a wearout level to where they had to look at new improvements. They ignored improvements. They took opportunities where monies that were being gained could have been invested, and they didn't do that. They went into other fields and projects and they failed. And because they failed, we suffered, and today again there is no contract, no contract in this country that's protecting its employees or its retirees for benefits negotiated if they hit the level of Chapter 11.

Now, my point here is that if the organized labor doesn't find some kind of language that protects that company from pulling that kind of protection from themselves so they can get away from legacy costs, they are all going to end up like we have ended up here today.

One other thing, the fact that the company went bankrupt doesn't necessarily mean they are not making a profit today, because they are under a different name without any legacy overhead. Now, that should not have been permissible here in this country. I don't care where they are from. If they are going to buy out an organization, then they have got to pick up the tab that put that operation there, and that's the kind of language of the law or legislation that should be developed and designed and put into effect.

Now if you want to shut Sparrows Point down, shut it down. They didn't shut Sparrows Point down. They just crippled it here and there, but they took the biggest cost that they promised these people who are out here now away from them, and that was benefits negotiated in good faith.

As far as women working in the mill, Well, you know, I wasn't there during the world war changes where women operated tractors and cranes. They did everything but operational on the mills. For whatever reason, they didn't get on the mills themselves, but they were tractor operators, they were crane operators and they were tin flippers. They weren't inspectors at that time. They were tin flippers, which is just temporary because of the war, like Rosie the Riveters. Exactly, that's a good term, because they were the Rosie the Riveters, and that was the function they took, but then it got halted and it took on a different prospect.

When I got there in '59, they used to have separate restaurants for the women, facilities naturally for the women, and the guys weren't permitted in certain areas in the mill where the women were and that's just the way it was. The change that I seen, the only change I seen, was where the shear floor -- not the shear floor as much as the tin flipping operation itself--was eliminated. It was eliminated. This is part of your job elimination where so many things are starting to come out of the closet. They designed this coil data recorders, which were inspectors, the girls that would get up in the booths while the coil was running and inspect that steel, and when that phase came into effect, that eliminated the sorting room, they didn't need the sorting room any more. That didn't happen overnight, it took a little while, but then the operations started to be eliminated, and the next thing, full coil forms at Sparrows Point was eliminated to square box form, which was the square deal. They ended up eliminating the shear floor period totally, there was no shears operating anywhere in the mill. There were something like 24 shears. The shears would cut the rolls to a specific length. They went from what I call box steel to coil form. Now, by making that transition, that change, that eliminated all that operation right there, and it's hindsight now because if you only had been able to see that beforehand, you wouldn't have made this change happen, you would have had other courses to take, but nobody saw that come that way. It was protecting profit over productivity and that phase of terminology.

Superintendent Franko Salona, he was a piece of work. Franko Salona came from Burns Harbor, came down here and became the superintendent of tin mill in the '70s. When he came down there and took over, the first thing he did was come out into the tin mill and he saw these scrap bales, which in his mind instantly was money-- "look at all that wasted steel." It's going to be scrap and sent over and melted down, and the first thing he did was demand that there be less bales of scrap, and there were precautions that were supposed to be taken, that that oversize slitting or narrow slitting, it wasn't necessary to slit so narrow. The narrower the better, put it that way. The narrower of the steel being split the better because that's less waste in his opinion.

No one really knew what was really intended behind the mindset of his thinking until after the shears were eliminated, because down the road he opened up an operation that took our pups, that was steel that would no longer be accepted by the customer. He would take the pups, and he would do exactly what number ten shear used to do, and that was to cut the pups up for scraps and melt it, that kind of thing, and that's what he did, and then he retired.

You can see -- I mean this guy, his point of vision was well ahead of itself because I guess being exposed out there in the steel world itself and to the greed that exists out there and the profit levels of steel productions for steel companies, he saw that and he took advantage it. So he retired, he's got an operation down there making money hand over foot over scrap pups that we used to make money on. We sent them to him now, or they did then. I don't know what they are doing now. They probably seen the same thing and they said, "The hell with this, we're not going to do that."

Yes, he started his own company and then retired. He started the company at a different location, and there were other concerns about some of the parts that were being sort of vandalized, whether that was going to his operation because of the cost of material and spare parts.

But all this started to take place, from the '70s and rolling into the '80s, and we are rolling into something that was really mishandled in my opinion, and I was crucified for my opinion, and that was the Consent Decree, if you want to get into that.

When I started working at The Point, there were then segregated bathrooms and locker rooms. There were no blacks in the tractor game. No, they were in labor gangs and they were in tractors and they were in cranes. Not many on production lines at all at that time. Maintenance had a few, yes. For what it's worth, most were on the steel side where the real hot jobs were, and I guess it's not a good term to use here but the most unsafe jobs were in that area. Local 2610 was maybe 65 to 70 percent black members. At least, and I guess that's the culture of it all.

Even when the homes used to be down there, they had their own -- you know, their bungalows and all. There was the blacks here and there was the whites there, so it was an actual culture that was developed there. Now what you just said is exactly what I said before. Even when I was kid, you never saw that differences of color. That's what you wanted to do and that's what they wanted to do. In fact, that words never entered my mind, "they" and "me." It was "us." They were black, we were white. As kids you don't even recognize the black and white part of it. As time went on, you can see all these other really ugly situations that existed and these campaigners that come out here, save us and we're the race that was discriminated. I'm Irish, my race was discriminated here. I mean this is just what evolved after all this other --

I think what really stirred it up was in the '60s. I think when the Civil Rights Act of '64 started to open up the doors for civil rights themselves, and then '68 really took a better, stronger stand, and things that were going on. People really didn't believe it was happening anyway because that generation of blacks didn't feel what was embedded in their thinking today. It wasn't there, and it way the way of life, it was America, this is the way it is and that's the way they grew up.

I wasn't back there when they were hanging the blacks and I wasn't there then, I don't even associate with doing that. I know the states, if you look at geography wide, there's states that really took advantage of the blacks, and in fact even went to Africa and got slaves and all that kind of stuff, and that was a condition that was here. It wasn't something that was created, other than the fact that it happened here.

But the Indian, we can go on a whole different train of thinking here. But culturewise, America is a diversity of many different cultures housed with one rule--Washington trying to implement laws that are offensive to some. Religion is another sensitive type area to get into discussions, because this religion is better than that religion, and I believe the Lord is here and I believe the Lord is coming, and we got so much diversity in thinking here, it's unbelievable.

When I started there, yes, locker rooms weresegregated. Integration came in the '60s. That's when things started to really show the fact that hey, this is discriminatory, you can't do that. Why? Well, the '64 civil rights, then '68. Well, prior to '64 there was none of that, and then, just like any kind of an adjustment, after you are sort of, I guess, accustomed to what was going on with black versus white and then, in

LeRoy McClelland, Rev. Oscar Hoggs, Lee Douglass at CCBC-Dundalk

your own mind you had this thought. In fact, now that you mention that, on North Point Road there are bars there, there was never a black person in there. They had a bar that they went in to called Mickey's, and it's like a restaurant bar type. It's still there to this day. That's where all the blacks went. Did they go there because there was no place else they could go? That could be, or did they go there because that's where they began to go to start with because they lived that sort of--this is the way it is and change is not going to happen.

I was raised with that kind of concept, I guess, but now that you mention something like that, that's another thing that hits you right square in the eyes, because the other bars--Uncle Louies, Pop's, the Whitehouse. Anyway, Uncle Louies was probably one of the most active besides Pop's Tavern, but there were all white people there. They were all -- some of the women, too by the way, but there's not as many women there, and the management uniquely used to go to what's called The Greenhouse, or something that was next to Pop's tavern.

That was all management. They wouldn't go to any other bars because of the association, management with union, it wasn't embraced. We used to be out there for a while and get a little toot on and say "let's go down there to the management bar," and we would, we would go in there, and as soon as you walk in the door, the guys would be there, they would be on the tables, "We're going to challenge you guys a game," and we sort of jump into their area, but you know what -- we even went down to the Sparrows Point Country Club. Yeah, not by invitation, we just went, and if it wouldn't have been for the cops-- at that time, there was a police force at Sparrows Point period, that isn't what it is today, rent a cop. These guys --I forget how we ended up going over there one time. It wasn't too well accepted, but it's a country club, and that even changed after years went by. They opened up the memberships to the hourly.

All in all, the wrongs were trying to be placed right. There was a reaction to how you went about doing that, and with the Consent Decree, that's where the government realized, whether they liked it or not, they had to make and face the change.

Prior to the Consent Decree, there was not a lot of discussion in the plant. I mean, I think what really started to surface is the civil rights part of it. I think some -- well, like Lee Douglass told you, there was no real ugly discrimination going on. This is just the way it is. Promotion was a big thing, and that fell in line not just with male, but female too, because there was never a female on the mills and then that door started to open so we had that opportunity there. Blacks started to get an opportunity to get on production jobs. They worked predominantly on the tractors and the cranes by the way-- I take it back, they were predominantly tractor operators. It was always white crane operators, and then production rollers and all, they were always white, they was never black. Blacks would either be scaleman or they would be pull tracers, you know those positions, and then naturally all this other thing started to surface, discriminatory and blah, blah, blah, I guess between the international union.

Keep in mind I'm a representative, I'm a zone committeeman, and when this thing started to come together, what it was created to do was really confusing to a lot of us. To me, it was just a blatant effort to cover up something that happened way back when hiring of black employees were going on, and nobody really looked at the matter.

Dave Wilson was still president, and, me being who I am, sometimes you put your foot in your mouth, sometimes you just got to bite it off, that's all there is to it. When I saw that coming down and I fought it. That's where I got with a bunch of guys around the plant, black and white together, male, too, female, I started to put an organization together called the Employees for Equal

Justice. That would be around '77, '76. The Consent Decree has already been issued and it stirred up so much dissension that the common sense just wasn't there any more. There were groups from outside, like CORE, which came down to the plant and picketed and leafletted and stuff like that and NAACP. It opened up all kinds of -- I guess it goes back to the squeaking wheel gets the grease philosophy, and then we started to see a lot of that. There were guys who were buddies -- that was another unique thing. We worked together, the tractor department, black, white together and never any kind of thoughts about after work. Never -- that might be an idea on my part, but I stop at the bar, Uncle Louis or Pop's, or any of them, I never dreamt of thinking about "Well, Robinson here who is black, he didn't stop." I never even thought that way. If that's what they wanted to do, that's what they did, not dreaming that they couldn't do it if they wanted to. I know that sounds stupid, but that's just the feeling that was there for eleven years.

The Consent Decree, its purpose was to actually justify what was and bring it up to date what is now going to be, but by implementing the Consent Decree, it caused more damage. It was a reverse discrimination case, period. Instead of it correcting something, it aggravated the situation, and that's what they did, it's pitting one against the other, that was the main. I'll give you an example. Most blacks were working in the locker rooms. The consent decree come out with this settlement, which a lot of blacks resented because of what it really meant. Why should that guy there who lived most of his work life in the locker room, now get this money for being denied to be on the mill when he's not at this point not even qualified? Why should that be an exception to the rule? That's what aggravated a lot of people right there in itself. And that thing just festered, it just got worse.

There was one against the other, and guys --Johnny Robertson and Hal, these are black | that I knew, they sort of stood away, they didn't want to talk any more, they just barred themselves. You are the enemy, okay. You are the redneck, and it really got ugly, it got ugly in a lot of ways. I used to come home here, my wife would be sitting around the table, I would say "You know I don't understand what's happening here." We are a union. Union means all of our members, black, white, male, female, but yet this is allowed to go on way back then. I mean you are talking in the '40s, this was allowed to be there then and now, suddenly, the generation that's here now are classified as being discriminated against? Well, if anyone that was discriminated against, it was back then in the '40s, not here. This was what was allowed to be.

So anyway, with the discrimination part of it, I got pretty bent out of it. I was going to even resign as a union representative because I couldn't get the support from the union, and the reason I couldn't get the support is because they were part of the Consent Decree.

I mean, the officers and the International, the district. See, the locals, the local unions sort of had their own powers, but naturally they had to answer to a higher power, and I can see it now because it's over with. There were those locally who contributed but didn't want to be recognized for it, and I accepted that. Quite a few of them, by the way, without mentioning names, but they might be embarrassed now, they had called me at home and said "LeRoy, you know the reasons that you are coming up with this new group and you know the International is not endorsing it. We know this, we understand it and we want to help you."

Here's how I started Steelworkers for Equal Justice. I got to talking to a few guys, and I said "Look, we're not going to be able to do something within the union, grievances ain't going to help." "Why isn't the grievance going to help?" Because it's an agreed-to Consent Decree, all parties agree. Well, the issue of getting in place was the big question, the leapfrogging is what we called it. I guess between unit seniority, department seniority and plant seniority, and this Consent Decree was an opportunity just to merge all three of them into one plant seniority.

And then the next issue in front of the plant seniority came white, black -- we're not worried about female. White, black, white, black, it was a percentage thing, and they were looking at different sections of the Sparrows Point operations which had more black than white and white than black and that kind of thing. So, they were sort of looking at that kind of schematic of how they were going to do this.

When they did fully implement the Consent Decree, it did violate promotional rights, it eliminated them, and that's where I got on this tangent of reverse discrimination. I got to talking to a few guys in, of all places, the bar, and they said "LeRoy, you are shooting a dead duck, it ain't going to happen." I said "Look, we don't know nothing unless we try it. Let's bring attention to this thing. Discrimination is heavy, it's out there, it's on everybody's lips." Well, have you ever heard the word "reverse discrimination?" Well, this discrimination is causing reverse discrimination. And then we went on the whole nine yards of this and that. Well, finally to make the organization legal, because I knew I was going to get heat, I was the chairman, then I had a treasurer, I had a secretary. The treasurer was -- I had the name on the end of my lips. Ernie Johnson, he was the treasurer. I don't know if he's still alive. I know he retired. He took -- I think he took the lump sum. Ernie Johnson. Then I had a guy by the name of Rogers who was black, he was the secretary.

It was our purpose to have a mixed-race group. Our whole issues were focused on the same object really and what we said, "Now, here's black, he's in a job. Why should I have to give up my job to that guy in the locker room because he's black?" Now, we have a plant seniority. To get into a unit, you have to fit into that department and then you have these exercises. This was what this was all about, and I think in all mindset I think they looked at that as sort of a lateral discrimination because he didn't want the job at that time. So, they got the job in the locker room. It was laid back type of uptown job.

So as this thing started to get uglier, and me particularly I spent all my time in the tractor department. So, we have a white guy now, this ain't black, this is white. He comes out of the warehouse with his seniority, gets to leap frog over top of me in my unit, and I screamed "How can that happen?" And then we got all this happening around us. I said "Look, we can talk all we want, okay, it's like talking in the wind. Let's create a group, let's get it legalized" because the IRS and all this other -- I know it's going to be turned into this "What are we doing" or "Is this a scam?" or what we are doing here because we are handling other monies and every nickel had to be accounted for. So, we do all this, and we get a pretty good group.

I hold the meeting, and we get people who came up --we had the first meeting up in our own union hall, unbeknownst to certain individuals we had it, and we had a pretty good turnout. At that time I guess it was 50, 70 people, and we were talking, black, white, male, female. We were talking exactly where we thought we could go with this, and I said "We all know in this room we can't turn to our international union, we can't turn to our local union because they are all part of the Consent Decree. We can't turn to anybody in the government, like the NLRB, we can't do any of that because the government is part of the agreement, and the company is part of the agreement."

So what I'm going to do is find us a lawyer that will handle it. Well, that wasn't easy to do because no lawyer wanted to handle the Consent Decree, because they knew that it was already a binding agreement between all three parties, so how are you going to fight that issue? My concern was, if we're not fighting the discrimination, we are fighting the reverse discrimination. I couldn't get them to separate the thinking on that.

Charles Lee Nutt, he just happened to pop up. One of the guys were going to Dundalk College, Community College, and his name come up. Ed Angelo, he was the other one that was part of our group. He was a roller on the tandem mill. He used to live in Kingsville. Anyways, we get introduced to Charles Lee Nutt, and Charles impressed me immensely because other lawyers that we thought were going to take this case and just didn't want to have anything to do with it. He says "Well, let me tell you guys something," this is him speaking before we passed on. He says "I came to Baltimore without a penny. I can leave Baltimore without a penny." That's sort of his comment. He said "But I want to tell you guys something right now. First off, it's not going to be easy, it's going to be costly and there's no guarantee, but I will take it on," and we did. We went through our court. We went through the Appeals Court and we are sitting and waiting for the Supreme Court. Oh, yes, this took several years. It was probably in the '80s, '83, somewhere in there.

There was some backlash in the shop, including some of the local officers. Some of them. Well, some of them were just guys at that time, some of them were so dedicated to the International, looking for a staff job that they just didn't want to have their actual true feelings known. But there were others like I am telling you who had told me in confidence, and I respect that and they give me their money-- we started off getting donations of $50. You don't think that wasn't tough, but we did, and then we held raffles, things like that, to keep the money flowing for the litigation.

Anyway, it got all the way down to the point to the Supreme Court, and then Charles gets this response that the Supreme Court will not hear the case, and I was confused by that. How can they not hear this case? We have gone through all the procedures, we've gone all through the courts, how can they deny us?

Well, we all had a meeting-- at East Point, at one of the restaurants down there, and we all are sitting down there, and as soon as I seen him [Nutt] walk in the door, I knew that it ain't going to be good news. So, he went ahead and he told us it wouldn't be accepted, and he had said from the beginning, and I can't argue with it, didn't argue with it, that he said it would be a tough road to hoe, no guarantees. But my comment then from the beginning was "nothing ventured, nothing gained." We've got to do something. This is so clear to me, and I'm an average person. How in the hell can something discriminatory not be reverse discrimination, because this is what it is? Look at the repercussions and stuff, look what's happened, look at the leap frog, look at the -- not security, but the seniority practices that were in place for so many years for job protection, for promotions and things like that. That's all dissolved. How can it just happen like that? It affects us directly and that's discrimination.

So anyway, it all come to an end and some of the guys will never let me forget it. "I told you, I told you." I said "All right, you told me. Now I am telling you this, at least we tried," and we moved on."

I think those who cashed their checks just took that as "you are going to give it to me, I'm going to spend it." Did it change them? No. Did they accept that? No.

There was a large number who refused to cash their checks, yeah, and that was supposed to send a signal, too, and we had black representatives, by the way in the staff. Bernie Parish. They, too -- I can't speak for either of them, but they, too, within their own organization dealt with it, I guess, as effectively as they could, but like any organization, there's control. It is what we are today. It's a shame that all these relationships that, through the years, we developed and these challenges that we faced, the guys that were really instrumental in it, you don't see or hear from any more. The only time I get to do what I want to do, and I like it, don't get me wrong, I do miss not getting them phone calls and the conditions that exist. I do miss the challenges. It's taken a lot of adjustment to do that, but I found the relief by putting some of my feelings in an article and challenging somebody's comment about this and that.

Outsourcing is a sore spot with me now. Healthcare is a sore spot with me. Food bank, you've been on the food bank a lot time, Harvest for the Hungry. Why should that even exist in this country? Now we've got this big -- it's going to be bigger than anybody realizes, this Latino, the illegal immigration going to be a big, big issue. It shouldn't shock anybody to know what I had said before--the squealing wheel gets the oil, and they are going to be squealing enough to where they are going to make exceptions to the rule. When they make exceptions to the rule, there's diminution, it's over, it's done.

So, change is inevitable, it's there. You may not like to hear some of the things that are being said, but the competition is globalization. If we don't really learn what that really means in America here, we're going to end up being the American warehouse for foreign products. Again, I already fall back on this, I fall back on the fact that I don't know any other English than the English that I was born and raised with, but I am confused when I hear some Spanish someone standing in front of me in line, spouting off, whether they are talking about me or what they are doing, I don't understand, but they understand us, and that's frightening in itself, too.

If I had to do it over again would I? Truthfully? No. If I had to do it over again, I would have done what my mother told me to do, to stay in the Navy. I would have retired from the Navy. In fact, that was part of my life that started off when I was 17-years old and reciprocating engines -- I don't know how familiar you are with the terms I'm going to use here, but the reciprocating engines are what propelled our aircraft, blimps, everything was propeller driven. Then as time went on and in the latter part of years where jet engines become the propulsion system, all that came really to open up to me the production station. They had all these jets and propeller type of things that they were experimenting with, because it was an experimental situation and you got to see that, the beginning of it. You got to see the testing, and here I sit going on age 69, seeing it put to action on the TV, seeing the self-propelled hardware. It's fascinating, and to think that some of the things that I have seen as I got older, you would think I would be 150 years old with the changes, but I just happened to be in that period of time where these things were going on, gas lights to electric, from black and white TV round to color TV. VCRs, CDs. It's like damn, what more can be said?

Oh, my God, yeah. My mom is 92 and can go all the way back. Now you are talking time when the war was a big issue. My dad didn't go into the war because he had so many kids, he was exempt from the war. I guess anybody you would really sit down and talk to has a lot to say about their individual life and experiences, and that's fascinating in itself.

How would my life be different if I stayed in the Navy? Well, a couple things I thought about. I wouldn't have the kids I had because we would be moving from base to base. With me, I went from Norfolk, Virginia, to Gitmo City, the VU10 squadron. What our purpose down there was we had the B25s, we had the F5Fs and F6 hellcats and the F9F jets, and with the reciprocating engines, we would tow targets for the fleet so that the destroyers would be able to take their target practice, and we would tow that target up there.

Well, my first time up there I was a towman, which meant I'm the one that pulled out the cable so they could shoot at it. Well, here's a B25. If you can imagine, a B25, double engine. We are up there, already got air pockets up and down, oh gees, and then boom, you hear the repercussions where the shell come up and hit the target, which is 200 feet away from the aircraft, but it hit that target, and the repercussion, the plane went like that. Oh, my God, we're hit, we are hit, we are hit. And the pilot up there, the lieutenant hollered back, "Hey, look, just sit back and just let the cable go, okay. We'll handle the ship." And then we get down and I couldn't eat. We had supper. I couldn't even eat supper, I was so upset.

Well, I guess the other side of that, not doing it all over again, I guess the other side is exactly what you would miss, because that's what my life is right now, that's what got me -- as I was already quoted as an angry old man. Yeah, I'm angry. I'm angry at a lot of things that shouldn't have to be. I'm angry at the fact that here I have three grandsons and I'm sitting here with a life stolen question whether tomorrow we are going to sell this house just to exist or whether my Medicare is going to run out. Sure, if I had to do it over again, I would look into that, and the reason I am saying that, and that's hindsight, because I know what was already, so I don't know what would have been there, except I would have a pension that would not be questionable. My health benefits, which through the VA would not be questionable, even for my wife I provided for under retirement because it's a tri-state type of healthcare. I'm a VA, a veteran now, I get the benefits of a prescription program, I get the benefit of going down there for a checkup, but I don't get the other perks that may be available if I was wounded. God help me, I wasn't wounded, but I just feel that's a little bit discriminatory, too. You served your country, you spent your four years over there, you were in the same places that guys lost their lives and arms and what have you, but you were lucky enough not to be one of them. But then you come back, you don't get the benefit of those benefits in total. Parts of it, piece of this and piece of that. That's another part of life.

The union by the way--I will end it this way. I loved the union, I loved the direction that it has to take and the change, and I question if those in positions have the ability to make those decisions. That's the bigger question that comes out of my mind, because it is what I said. Outsourcing is going to cripple this country, it's going to cripple organized labor, and if organized labor doesn't become one solid organization to where you can feel the power that the immigrants are going to show today--when you see on TV and what power across this country can do and how you can cripple the politicians with power of those who, like us retirees, have with our vote.

There's so many different versions of what hits you strongly and what doesn't hit you. Well, really, it's not one thing I can focus on. I think the thing that I look forward to, and this might be odd for some people to hear, I looked forward to going to work. I enjoyed it, I enjoyed every day in the mill as I enjoyed every day at that union hall. Even though there were hostile feelings and there was arguments, but it makes you feel like you are a part of it. The union gives me an identity of where I spent my life. I'm a retired steelworker, very proud to be a retired steelworker. If I retired from the Navy, I would have been a very proud -- I'm still proud of my service time, but I would have been a proud Navy person, military person, respectful of our people over there right now giving their lives up for a war that should not be, lives lost for a war that should not be. Here we sit, we are looking at gas prices going up, we are looking at electricity going up. It's just something else. I mean it's an experience I guess to live it, to be able to talk about it and then be able to see it on tape will be an experience in itself.

As for whether I wanted my son working at The Point, well, I did and I didn't. It's a choice he made. I did what my dad said to me, "You make the choice." In fact, he had that old saying of you make your bed, you've got to lie in it. Well, that's what he wanted, that's what he got and he's a good production worker. Again, like I said, it's not too long ago, he was talking about the group and they want to eliminate a solution tech who is part of that group. Well, the solution part now is taken over by technology, so you don't need that kind of a balance, they do it automatic now. So naturally the company is not going to keep another person just to stand by.

That's not going to happen. That's why technology takes the jobs. He was sort of confused about where he stood. "Dad, I'm here to make money, that's what I am there for." I understand that. The company is there to make a profit, but we are there to share the wealth, and that's what we are supposed to be. If you can't share the wealth with the crew that you are working with and you lose respect in your own group, you are going to be a man without a helmet.

Well, I think the better part of what was more pertaining to why he has this lackadaisical attitude towards being more involved in the union is what they did to me, and it isn't the union, and I keep trying to get that in their head. It isn't the union that did this to me. It's the companies and the Decree out there that did this, and then they throw out a couple comments as if to say "Well, if they would have taken some of your direction before, the union would still be stronger," but nobody saw that way. I said "John, you know I guess we are all human, we all look at what we think we can do to make things a lot stronger and better," but sometimes by preventing technology, it's defeating us to start with overall, That's not an easy decision to make, it isn't, and the union is going to make a decision somewhere down the line or they are going to get the attitude like my son has got and other younger workers right now--they don't see the need. But there is always going to be a need for organized labor--always. I'm very proud to be a member of SOAR, and this organization is going to reactivate the sleeping majority of retirees. Amen.

In the spring, 2018, Kevin Sheets, who grew up in North Point Village and graduated from Sparrows Point High School and now teaches history at SUNY Courtland, excerpted part of this transcript for his book, *Sources For American History, Vol. 2: Since 1865.*" The excerpts, pp. 110-112, and 114-115 of this chapter, are placed between interviews with Irving Kristol, talking about Free Market Capitalism, and Bill Clinton, endorsing The North American Free Trade Agreement (NAFTA).

Sheets sent a copy of the book to LeRoy, who read it on his front porch in late summer, 2018.

GLOSSARY

As I did the interviews for this book, it was clear that the workers at Sparrows Point have a special language for people, processes and locations, both in the mill and in the community. In a line that is not in these interviews, I say:

MR. BARRY: "One of the things that has always concerned me about different interviews that people do and the classes that we do that these are going to be shown to people who have never been to Bethlehem Steel, and they need to have a better sense of exactly what you talk about, the terminology of the men and the women. You are going to have people who are outside the industry, and so I'm just going to ask you to kind of describe it for the people who are going want to watch this."

So this glossary, prepared with great help from Don Kellner and Chris MacLarion, tries to help you out.

56—cold sheet metal--56" HSM slab reheat furnaces. As a cold slab was charged (pushed) into the back of the reheat furnace, the entire contents of the furnace was pushed forward until one hot slab would fall out onto the delivery tables, slide up a "bumper" and fall back to the tables. The hot slabs sliding across the furnace skids or solid hearth could be damaged on the underside during the "push." Skid damage and the drop out sequence were significant sources of gouge and sliver type defects, particularly for cold rolled or tin products.

42 mill and the 48—in the tin mill

68 mill---the hot strip mill was the first procedure on the finishing side, opened in 1947

Amoco—a bar

BJ department—included the entire tin mill production (including the 42 and the 48 mills)

BL department—the 56" cold mill

BP department—the 68" hot strip mill

BOF--Basic Oxygen Furnace was Blast furnace

Bull gang—the classification of skilled workers who did complicated repair jobs throughout the whole works. Each mill had its own separate bull gang. In later years the individual mill "bull gangs" were done away with and there was one large plantwide bull gang who would go mill to mill on "outage" days to help do the work individual mill maintenance crews couldn't handle alone

CA (Continuous Annealing) line was part of the tin mill

CDR girl—Cold Data Recorder, in the tin mill, to measure the size of the coil, the finished product

Coils—the finished product after the steel was finished (Picture a 50,000 roll of steel toilet paper. That was a coil)

Electrical Department—each mill had its own group of electricians, but the 458 Department covered the whole works

Electroplate line—in the Tin Mill, applied plating to tin as a customer specified

ERS—Electrical Repair Shop on the steel side which did the big bulk work for electronics

Expediter—most of the mills had one, whose job was to check to see if new material was needed

Feeder—sent the slabs of steel through the finishing mills The feeder also fed coils of steel through Tandem and Skin Mills

Glenn L. Martin—an aircraft manufacturer in Essex, MD, an important part of "industrial" Baltimore

Hallogen line—coated the steel in the Tin Mill—the BH Department

Don Kellner—longtime president of Local 2609 and the president of the Steelworker Retirees

Labor Gang—each mill had a group of unskilled workers, and there was also a plant-wide group which could be assigned to any mill. Labor Gangs were largely done away with after the Bethlehem Steel bankruptcy in 2001.

Legacy costs—the obligation for the company to pay for pensions and health care for retired workers. The union negotiated a 30-year and out contract so many workers could retire at a relatively young age. When Bethlehem Steel declared bankruptcy in 2001, it cancelled all of these payments, leaving many workers—both production and salaried—without health insurance.

Local 2610—one of five locals at The Point, this local covered the steel side, where the raw product was forged

Local 2609—this local covered the finishing side, where special coatings, like tin, were added to the steel

Local 9116—this local represented the clerical and technical workers

Chris Loucas—started working at Sparrows Point in 1936 and was president of Local 2609 from 1950-56 and retired in 1964.

David McDonald—originally the Secretary-Treasurer in 1936 of the Steelworkers Organizing Committee (SWOC), he became president of the union from 1953-1965. and retired in 1964.

Mechanical Department—the group did the repair work, and each mill had its own Mechanical Department, and there was also one for the whole works.

422 Mechanical Department—maintained the equipment in the hot strip mill

Mickeys—is a store and bar on the east side of North Point Blvd, located so workers on their way home would pass it on the divided highway. It cashed checks for workers, including black workers, and became a famous gathering place.

Mobile equipment--- Mobile Equipment was a plant wide department/unit under Local 2610 that managed all of the plant's equipment from bulldozers and dump trucks to mobile cranes needed during mill outages.

Nail mill—one of the original mills at Sparrows Point, this mill was shut down in the 1980's

Bill Nugent—started at Sparrows Point in 1965, became an officer of Local 2609 and then became Assistant to District 8 Director Dave Wilson. Nugent ran for District Director and lost to the current Director, Ernest "Billy" Thompson in 1998.

Patapsco and Back River Railroad—the railroad inside the mill, whose workers were represented by a steelworkers local.

Pennwood Power—the central plant that produced electricity for the mill

Pickler—this process cleaned the steel coming out of the Hot Strip mill and added covering for the sheet steel in both the tin mill and the sheet metal mill.

Ed Plato—officer of USWA District 8

Prep line—in the tin mill, this process sliced steel down according to a customer's order

Shears/shear floor—a unit in the Tin Mill which cut the steel to a customer's order

SIP—Social Insurance Program, negotiated by the union, SIP was an insurance payment where a worker could get a weekly check if out sick or hurt in a non-work-related event.

"steel side"—the section of the mill where steel was initially forged, before being sent to the "finishing side."

Sweetener—additional money offered by Bethlehem Steel to supplement a pension to encourage workers to retire. When the company declared bankruptcy, all of the sweeteners were stopped.

Tandem department—3 units that processed the steel after it passed through the pickler

Tin mill—The finishing side of the plant where tin coating was applied to the steel for use in cans and other products. Originally called "the hot strip, it later became the original cold mill, (later the coating products division), then the New Cold Mill.

Wire mill—produced wire, later closed in the 1980's

Sewing room—where the steel was drawn in the rod and wire mill

Dave Wilson—first wife Marianne, second wife Dee Wilson—a member of Local 2609, who served two terms at District President.

Afterword

I started teaching union classes at Sparrows Point in 1999, in rooms at Career Development, a program negotiated by the Steelworkers Union to offer free education to any member. I was an instructor at Dundalk Community College (later part of The Community College of Baltimore County), located just up the road from the mill and part of the Sparrows Point community. While my classes were union skills--like grievance and arbitration, contract negotiations, and organizing--the participants, who came directly from work in the mill to the classes, talked steel. Their stories of their experiences in the mills, in their unions, and in their communities, were so exciting that I thought they needed to be recorded. They were participants in an epic civilization that is unfortunately only getting attention now that it is disappearing.

I started several years later to videotape the interviews so that workers could see—as well as hear—the steelworkers. When the mill closed in August, 2012, I was glad I had finished more than 80 interviews and I have continued to make new videos.

If you look at the dates of these interviews, you may wonder why it took so long to get them published. The answer to this, like the answer to so many things, is money—to pay for transcriptions. The skill of three transcribers, Shari Young, John Bailey and Johanna Seymour, is extraordinary and I appreciate the work they did.

One problem with talking steel is that it is a unique language with a special vocabulary. You could show these interviews to any steelworkers in the world and they would understand. For the rest us—not at all. The Glossary is hopefully enough of a "translation," but I worry that many of the *Bawlmer* references will not make sense.

As I prepared the transcripts for publication, I always feel a regret that I can't simply publish all these videos on-line so everyone could hear—and sense—the power of these workers. If you want to see more of this history, go to www.sparrowspointsteelworkers.com or look at the Facebook sites
- ✓ I Worked at Sparrows Point, https://www.facebook.com/I-Worked-At-Sparrows-Point-541445789271090/,
- ✓ USW Local 9477 Sparrows Point, https://www.facebook.com/groups/75860317772/ and
- ✓ I Grew Up in Sparrows Point, Md https://www.facebook.com/groups/264701639563/, administered by steelworker historian Elmer Hall.

Through this project, I have had great support: at CCBC from Dr. Avon Garrett and Dr. Tim Davis, who found money to pay for the first transcripts, and from David Forrest who guided me through all of the technical problems involved in recording with an old VHS camera that belonged to the college.

As I preserved old records from the union halls, Mike Lewis and Joe Benny, were helpful. I hope that some day there will be a Maryland Labor History Museum where all of this material can be displayed. I stored a lot of this material at the union hall, and when a pipe froze and broke,

Rob Schoberlein of the Baltimore City Archives stepped right up to provide both a secure location and enthusiastic support for saving steelworker history.

So many other people have joined in the steelworker history project that I can't list them all but a few are
- ✓ The Mill Stories project https://millstories.umbc.edu/, headed by Bill Shewbridge and Michelle Stefano, and
- ✓ Anthropology after The Wire http://anthropologybythewire.com/ directed by Matt Durington are two great projects, as is
- ✓ Keith Taylor's Sparrows Point/North Point Historical Society https://www.facebook.com/pg/spnphs/about/

And, as always, the biggest help came from Joan, Willie and Alex.

Bill Barry
March, 2019

Made in the USA
Middletown, DE
04 May 2019